How to Play Your Cards
When You Are the
DECLARER
At Contract Bridge

How to Play Your Cards When You Are the DECLARER At Contract Bridge

JOHN MALLON

Chilton Book Company *Radnor, Pennsylvania*

LIBRARY OF CONGRESS CATALOGING IN PUBLICATION DATA

Mallon, John.
How to play your cards when you are the declarer at
contract bridge.
1. Contract bridge.   I. Title.
GV1282.3.M3335   1976   795.4'15   76-5872
ISBN 0-8019-6446-6
ISBN 0-8019-6447-4 pbk.

Foreword

This book is offered as a text and reference book for learning and teaching How To Play Your Cards.

It presents clearly and concisely the fundamental principles and standard methods of play, which are based on common sense, mathematical probabilities, and the experience of generations of whist and bridge players.

Every effort has been made to make this study as easy as possible. Where bridge hands are shown, they can be visualized without effort, because they look like bridge hands. The material is logically arranged. Contrasting sizes and styles of type are used to make the essential instructions stand out so that they can be easily referred to and reviewed.

The instructions are stated positively as general rules which should be followed unless the bidding, the opening lead, or a previous play has given you information that warns you not to do so.

Exceptions to the general rules are given for situations which occur often enough to warrant mention. Situations that are seldom encountered or result only from freak hands are not included.

One very advanced play, the true squeeze, has been omitted deliberately. The chance to use it seldom comes up; and when it does arise, only the top experts seem able to recognize the opportunity in time to take advantage of it.

Anyone who understands the basic principles and follows the general rules explained in this book is sure to become a very fine bridge player.

I acknowledge with thanks the help I received from my neighbor, Mrs. Joseph Jones, who skillfully deciphered my handwriting and typed and edited my manuscript; from my friend Neville Blackemore and my wife, Eleanor, whose editing greatly improved its clarity; and from my friend William R. Phillips, one of

Louisville's very best bridge players, who corrected my errors in fact and judgment.

The words "always," "never," "sure," and "certain" do not really belong in the vocabulary of a bridge teacher or writer. Where they are found in this book, it should be understood that they are modified by the adverb "almost."

JOHN MALLON

Contents

PART II Summary

How to Play Your Cards
When You Are the
DECLARER
At Contract Bridge

Part I

HOW TO PLAY YOUR CARDS WHEN YOU ARE THE DECLARER

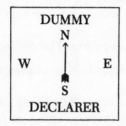

In the examples in this book, South is always the declarer, and you always hold the South hand.

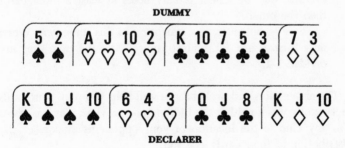

PERCENTAGES

A few simple facts are just about all you need to know about the Mathematics of Bridge.

1. **When your opponents hold only 1 honor in a suit:**
   50% of the time it is held by the opponent on your left, and 50% of the time by the opponent on your right.

   It is probably held by the opponent who holds the greater number of cards in the suit.

2. **When your opponents hold 2 honors in a suit:**
   50% of the time the 2 adverse honors are divided between your opponents.

   25% of the time both honors are held by the opponent on your left.

   25% of the time both are held by the opponent on your right.

3. **When your opponents hold an uneven number of cards in a suit:**
   The chances are about 2 to 1 that these cards are divided between your opponents as evenly as possible.

4. **When your opponents hold an even number of cards in a suit:**
   The chances are about 2 to 1 that these cards are not evenly divided. One opponent usually holds at least 2 more cards than the other.

   There is, however, one exception to this statement. When only 2 cards are out against you, 52% of the time they are divided 1-1.

The above facts and probabilities will help you play your cards successfully when neither the bidding nor previous play has given you any clue to the location of your opponents' honors or the distribution of their cards in a suit.

DISTRIBUTION OF CARDS
HELD BY OPPONENTS

You and Dummy Hold	Your Opponents Hold	Opponents' Cards are Divided	Approximate Percent of Time
11 cards	2 cards	1—1	52%
		2—0	48%
10 cards	3 cards	2—1	78%
		3—0	22%
9 cards	4 cards	3—1	50%
		2—2	40%
		4—0	10%
8 cards	5 cards	3—2	68%
		4—1	28%
		5—0	4%
7 cards	6 cards	4—2	48%
		3—3	36%
		5—1	15%
		6—0	1%
6 cards	7 cards	4—3	62%
		5—2	31%
		6—1	7%
		7—0	Nil

Don't try to memorize the above table. It is included here for reference only, to support the percentages mentioned on some of the pages in this book.

HOW TO TAKE TRICKS WITH LOW CARDS

Of the 13 tricks that are won in every deal, an average of 8 are won by honor cards, and 5 by low cards.

In order to make your contract you must usually establish low cards as winners in 1 or more of your long suits.

To develop a low card winner in a suit, you must continue to lead that suit until your opponents have played all their cards that are higher than your own low card(s).

You can seldom develop a low card winner in a suit in which you and the dummy together hold less than 7 cards.

When you hold 6 cards and your opponents hold 7 cards, as in Examples 1 and 2 below, you can never draw all your opponents' cards in 3 rounds of the suit. One of your opponents is sure to hold at least 4 cards.

Consequently, there is almost no chance that you can cash a low card trick on the fourth round.

There is, however a 62% chance that your opponents' cards are divided 4-3 and that you can draw all your opponents' cards in 4 rounds.

Therefore, if you can lead the suit 5 times, as in Example 2, you have a good chance to take a trick on the fifth round with a low card, even if it is the Two.

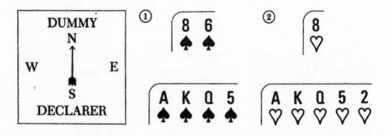

In the examples in this book, South is always the declarer and you are always South.

4

When you hold 7 cards and your opponents hold 6 cards, there is only a 36% chance that your opponents' cards are divided 3-3.

Consequently, when your 7 cards are divided 4-3, as they are in Example 3, the odds are about 2 to 1 that you cannot draw all your opponents' cards in 3 rounds and then be able to cash a low card trick on the fourth round.

There is, however, an 84% chance that your opponents' cards are divided either 3-3 or 4-2.

Therefore, if you can lead the suit 5 times, as you can in Example 4, you have a very fine chance to draw all their cards in 4 rounds and take a trick with a low card on the fifth round, even if it is the Two.

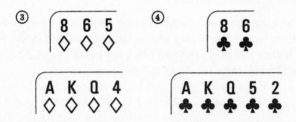

When you hold 8 cards and your opponents hold 5 cards, as in Examples 5 and 6, there is a 68% chance that your opponents' cards are divided 3-2.

Therefore, the odds are about 2 to 1 that you can draw all their cards in 3 rounds and thus take a low card trick on the fourth round.

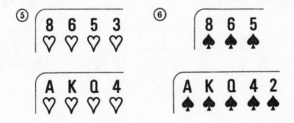

HOW TO TAKE TRICKS WITH HONORS OF EQUAL VALUE

When the 3 top honors in a suit are divided between your hand and the dummy, as in Examples 1 and 2, all your honors will take tricks.

When you and the dummy hold a solid sequence of honors, while your opponents hold 1 or more higher honors, as in Example 3, you may have to sacrifice 1 of your honors every time you drive out one of your opponents' higher honors. After that, each of your remaining honors will take a trick.

Whenever one hand contains more cards in the suit than does the other, be careful to play all the honors you hold in the shorter hand before you play your last low card in that hand. In this way you will keep from blocking the suit.

If, as in Example 1, in one hand you hold only 1 honor, and it is the top of the doubleton, play that honor on the first round of the suit.

If, as in Example 2, in one hand you hold 1 honor together with 2 low cards, play that honor on either the first or second round.

In Example 3 play dummy's Queen and Ten on the first 2 rounds of the suit.

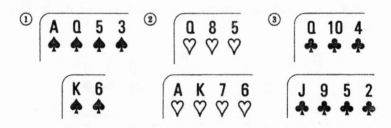

6

THE INDIRECT FINESSE—
A DEFENSIVE PLAY

You make an indirect finesse if you try to take a trick with a card you hold and prevent your opponents from capturing it when they hold a higher card in the same suit.

> The card you "finesse" is the card with which you try to take the trick.
> The card you "finesse against" is the higher card your opponents hold.

When you hold an honor, and your opponents hold a higher honor in the same suit, if you lead your honor, your opponents can always prevent it from taking a trick by covering it with their higher honor. But there is a 50% chance that your honor will take a trick if you lead a low card from the opposite hand up to your honor. When you do this, you make an "Indirect Finesse."

INDIRECT FINESSE
AGAINST AN ACE

You make an indirect finesse in its simplest form when, as in Example 1, you lead up to the King in the opposite hand, and finesse the King against the Ace.

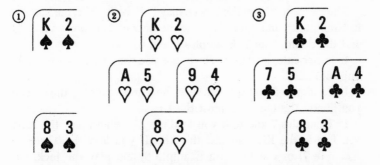

Half the time West will hold the Ace, as in Example 2, and your King will take a trick if you lead a low card from South's hand. Half the time East will hold the Ace, as in Example 3, and your finesse will fail.

Although there is a 50% chance that your finesse will fail, you are not really risking anything. If the card you are finessing against is on the wrong side, your card cannot win a trick, no matter how you play it.

The indirect finesse is a defensive play by which you hope to avoid losing a trick. You hope that the card you are finessing against is favorably located and that your honor will not be captured.

When you hold a sequence of honors in 1 hand, such as the King-Queen in Example 4, if possible, lead from the weak hand toward the strong hand each time you lead the suit until the Ace has been played.

If East holds the Ace, all of your honors will probably take tricks.

If you lead one of your honors before the Ace has been played, that honor can always be captured, no matter where the Ace is located.

④
```
7   4   3
♡   ♡   ♡

K   Q   8   6
♡   ♡   ♡   ♡
```

INDIRECT FINESSE AGAINST A KING OR QUEEN

A finesse is frequently based on a tenace holding, such as Ace-Queen, King-Jack, or Queen-Ten.

The cards that form the tenace may both be in the same hand, as in Examples 5 and 7, or they may be divided between your hand and the dummy, as in Examples 6 and 8.

In either case, lead up to the honor you want to finesse from the opposite hand.

In Examples 5 and 6 if you lead the Three and play the Queen, you finesse the Queen against the King.

In Examples 7 and 8, if you lead the Three and play the King, you finesse the King against the Ace. If you lead the Three (in Example 7) or the Four (in Example 8) and play the Jack, you finesse the Jack against both the Queen and the Ace.

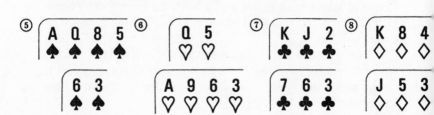

⑤
```
A   Q   8   5
♠   ♠   ♠   ♠

6   3
♠   ♠
```

⑥
```
Q   5
♡   ♡

A   9   6   3
♡   ♡   ♡   ♡
```

⑦
```
K   J   2
♣   ♣   ♣

7   6   3
♣   ♣   ♣
```

⑧
```
K   8   4
♢   ♢   ♢

J   5   3
♢   ♢   ♢
```

THE DIRECT FINESSE—
AN ATTACKING PLAY

The direct finesse is an attacking play whereby you try to capture an honor your opponents hold and prevent it from taking a trick.

DIRECT FINESSE AGAINST A KING

You make a direct finesse against a King when, as in Examples 1, 2, and 3, you lead an honor lower than the King from the hand opposite your Ace. You hope that your opponent who plays second hand will cover the honor you lead with his King, so that you in turn can capture his King with your Ace.

If the card you lead is not covered, do not play your Ace. Let your honor ride through for a finesse against the King.

In Example 1 lead the Queen. In Example 2 lead the Jack. In Example 3 lead the Ten.

① A 8 5 2 ♠ ♠ ♠ ♠

② A Q 8 2 ♡ ♡ ♡ ♡

③ A Q J 9 ♣ ♣ ♣ ♣

Q J 10 4 ♠ ♠ ♠ ♠

J 10 5 3 ♡ ♡ ♡ ♡

10 5 3 2 ♣ ♣ ♣ ♣

You deliberately sacrifice the card you lead. It can either be covered by the opponent on your left or captured by the one on your right.

As a general rule, try a direct finesse against a King only when you and the dummy together hold 4 of the 5 honors in the suit; that is, when you hold all the honors except the King.

When you hold 4 honors, you can expect them to take 3 tricks no matter how you play them. But if you make a direct finesse, and the King is where you hope to find it, you will take your 3 honor tricks without losing a trick and without giving up the lead; you will almost always capture the King.

9

When you hold only 3 honors (the Ace, Queen, and Jack) and your opponents hold both the King and the Ten, as in Examples 4 and 5, do not try a direct finesse.

You will take tricks with only 2 of your honors if you lead 1 of them.

Take for instance Examples 4 and 5. If you lead the Queen, it cannot take a trick, no matter which opponent covers it with the King. It can be covered in Example 4 and captured in Example 5. In both situations your opponents' Ten will control the third round of the suit.

For a direct finesse to be profitable, after the first round you must still hold the 2 highest cards left in the suit.

Consequently, when your opponents hold both the King and the Ten, as a general rule try an indirect finesse. Lead a low card from the opposite hand and finesse the Queen or Jack.

Half the time you will find the King favorably located as in Example 5; and whenever you do you will be able to establish all three of your honors.

④

A 6 4 2
♣ ♣ ♣ ♣

K 10 8   9 7 3
♣ ♣ ♣   ♣ ♣ ♣

Q J 5
♣ ♣ ♣

⑤

A 6 4 2
♦ ♦ ♦ ♦

9 7 3   K 10 8
♦ ♦ ♦   ♦ ♦ ♦

Q J 5
♦ ♦ ♦

EXCEPTIONS TO THE GENERAL RULE

When you hold the Ace, Queen, and Jack, and your opponents hold the King and the Ten, occasionally you should disregard the general rule.

When you hold the Ace-Queen-Jack, and your opponents hold the King and the Ten, you make a direct finesse against the King in the following situations.

1. Two tricks in the suit are all you need to make your contract.

2. You have a doubleton in the suit in your hand or in the dummy and can trump the third round, as in Examples 6 and 7.

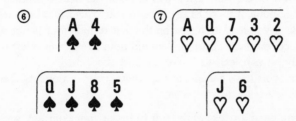

3. You hold the Ace, Queen, and Jack but not the Ten. You do, however, hold the Nine. These cards are distributed between your hand and the dummy as in Examples 8, 9, and 10.

On the first round lead the Queen or Jack toward the Ace.

If the honor you lead is not covered by the second hand opponent, but is captured with the King by the fourth hand opponent, you will still hold the 2 highest cards left in the suit.

If, however, your honor is covered by the King, which in turn is captured by your Ace, you will still hold a Queen-Nine or a Jack-Nine tenace in one hand.

On the second round you can lead up to this tenace and finesse the Nine against your opponents' Ten.

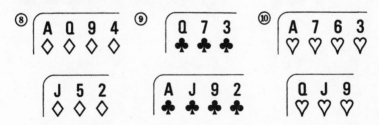

As a general rule, do not try a direct finesse when your Ace, Queen, Jack, and Nine are distributed between the 2 hands as in Examples 11, 12, and 13.

If you lead the Queen (Examples 12 and 13) or the Jack (Example 11) and your card is covered by the King, your Ace will take the first trick and your remaining honor will take the second trick.

If the honor you lead is not covered but is captured by your fourth hand opponent's King, you will then hold the 2 highest cards left in the suit. They will control the next 2 rounds.

But in none of these Examples can you expect to take more than 2 tricks if you lead an honor on the first round. Your honor will be either covered or captured. You will not have a tenace left toward which you can lead to finesse against the Ten.

After you have taken your 2 tricks, your opponents' Ten will almost always control the suit.

If you need 3 tricks in the suit to make your contract, your best hope is to try an indirect finesse. On the first round lead low toward the Jack or Queen opposite the Ace.

If the Ten is held by the opponent who plays before you play your Nine, and he plays low, your Nine will force out the King. Then your Ace, Queen, and Jack will be the 3 highest cards in the suit.

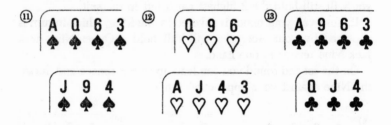

DIRECT FINESSE AGAINST A QUEEN

When you and the dummy together hold all the honors in a suit except the Queen, as in Examples 1 and 2, try a direct finesse against the Queen. Lead the Jack from the hand opposite your Ace or King.

When the Queen is favorably located, as it is in Example 1, you may expect to take 3 tricks with your honors without losing the lead.

When the Queen is unfavorably located, as it is in Example 2, it will capture your Jack, but you will then have the 3 highest cards left in the suit.

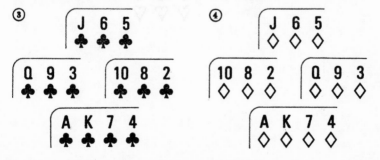

Do not try a direct finesse when your opponents hold both the Queen and the Ten, as in Examples 3 and 4.

If you lead your Jack, your opponents can prevent it from taking a trick no matter where the Queen is located. Then you cannot take more than 2 tricks with your honors. Your opponents' Ten will control the third round.

If, however, you try an indirect finesse and lead a low card toward the Jack, half the time you will find the Queen favorably located, as it is in Example 3. When you do, you may expect to cash your Jack as well as your Ace and King.

HOW TO LEAD TO A
DIRECT FINESSE

When you make a direct finesse, and the opponent on your left holds the honor you want to capture, occasionally his honor is well guarded, as it is in Example 1. In that case he may not cover the card you lead. He will allow it to take the trick.

When that happens, you want to make another direct finesse on the second round of the suit.

You may be able to do this, even when there are no entries left in the hand from which you lead, if on the first round you **lead the lowest card with which you can make a direct finesse, not the highest.**

For instance—in Example 1, lead the Nine on the first round, not the Jack. If the Nine holds, lead the Jack on the second round. If the Jack holds, lead the Four on the third round and finesse with the Queen. In this way you can finesse 3 times against the King, even when you have no entries in the South hand.

If you lead your Jack on the first round, and it holds, you will be unable to make a direct finesse on the second round. You will have to make an indirect finesse instead. Then, unless you have an entry to the South hand, you will be unable to finesse against the King a third time.

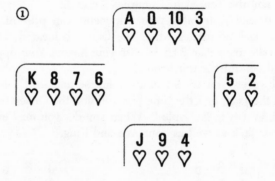

14

PLAY FOR A DROP

WHEN YOU WANT TO CAPTURE THE KING

1. **When you and the dummy between you hold 11 cards in a suit** with only 2 cards out against you, 1 of which is the King, as in Example 1, the King will be a singleton 52% of the time. So, more often than not, the King will be unguarded and will fall if you play your Ace on the first round of the suit.

   But the odds in favor of a drop are so slight that frequently it is wise to disregard them and to finesse against the King.

   For instance, a finesse is advisable under circumstances such as the following.

   a. When you have the slightest suspicion that the King is held by the opponent who must play second hand to the trick.

   b. When there is some reason why you cannot afford to let the opponent who plays second hand get the lead.

2. **When you and the dummy between you hold 10 cards** with only 3 cards out against you, one of which is the King, as in Example 2, do not play for a drop.

   The King will fall only 26% of the time.

   A finesse is almost always the best play. It will succeed 50% of the time. It will lose to a singleton King only 13% of the time.

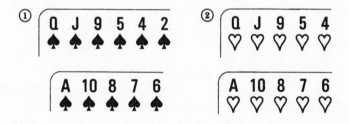

15

WHEN YOU WANT TO
CAPTURE THE QUEEN

When you and the dummy hold the Ace and King, while your opponents hold the Queen, the general rule is Eight Ever—Nine Never. This means that if you hold 8 cards in the suit, finesse against the Queen. If you hold 9 cards in the suit, play to drop the Queen.

When you hold 8 cards, as in Example 3, a finesse is usually the best play.

If you play for a drop, the Queen will fall only 34% of the time.

A finesse will succeed 50% of the time. It will lose 50% of the time, but only 17% of the time will it lose to a singleton or doubleton Queen that would have dropped if you had led out your Ace and King.

When you hold 9 cards, as in Example 4, the odds favor slightly a play to drop the Queen.

If you play your Ace and King on the first 2 rounds of the suit, the Queen will fall 52% of the time. It will not drop 48% of the time. But only 24% of the time will you fail to drop a Queen that you could have captured by finessing against it.

③
9	8	7	5
◇	◇	◇	◇

A	K	J	3
◇	◇	◇	◇

④
9	8	7	5
♣	♣	♣	♣

A	K	J	3	2
♣	♣	♣	♣	♣

EXCEPTIONS TO NINE NEVER

Because the odds in favor of dropping the Queen are so slight, it is frequently wise to disregard the general rule *Nine Never*.

It is advisable to finesse against the Queen under circumstances such as the following:

a. The bidding has indicated that the Queen is held by the opponent who must play second hand to the trick.

b. You cannot afford to let the opponent who plays second hand get the lead.

When you hold 9 cards headed by Ace-King, but your opponents hold both the Queen and Jack, as in Example 5, your best chance to capture both the Queen and the Jack is to lead out your Ace and King, even though the 4 cards your opponents hold will be divided 2-2 only 40% of the time.

If, however, one of your opponents drops the Jack or Queen on the first round of the suit, the chances are that it is a singleton and that the other opponent holds the second honor, guarded.

Therefore, when this happens, change your tactics and finesse against the honor that is still outstanding if it is possible to do so.

EXCEPTIONS TO EIGHT EVER

When you and the dummy hold 8 cards in a suit, with the Ace and King in one hand and the Jack in the other, while your opponents hold 5 cards including both the Queen and the Ten, as in Example 6, do not finesse against the Queen.

If you lead low toward the Jack, your opponents' Queen can take a trick 100% of the time.

Therefore, disregard the rule *Eight Ever* and lead out your Ace and King. There is a 33% chance that the Queen will fall. A 33% chance is better than no chance at all.

Moreover, even when the Queen does not fall, you have kept the lead and can shift to some other suit.

If it is the trump suit you have been playing, you may be able to force your opponents to trump another suit with their Queen and thus keep them from using it to capture 2 of your remaining trumps.

⑤ A K 10 7 6 ♠ ♠ ♠ ♠ ♠

⑥ J 8 7 ♡ ♡ ♡

9 4 3 2 ♠ ♠ ♠ ♠

A K 5 4 3 ♡ ♡ ♡ ♡ ♡

WHEN YOU WANT TO CAPTURE THE JACK

Sometimes the 3 top honors (Ace, King, and Queen) are divided between your hand and the dummy, while your opponents hold the Jack, as in Examples 7 and 8.

When you hold 10 cards in the suit, the Jack will fall if you lead out the Ace, King, and Queen.

When you hold less than 10 cards, you cannot be certain that the Jack will fall.

But even when the Jack is adequately guarded, you can make a safety play that may enable you to capture it.

As a general rule, on the first round of the suit play an honor from the hand that holds 2 of the 3 top honors. The cards your opponents play on the first round of the suit may give you a clue to the location of the Jack. If they do, you will still have a top honor in each hand, and you will be able to finesse against the Jack in either direction you choose.

For instance, in Example 7, play the King on the first round. If one of your opponents does not follow suit, you know that the other opponent holds the Jack, guarded. Finesse against it.

In Example 8, play the King on the first round. If both opponents play low, you have no clue. So play another honor from either hand you choose. The chances are that the distribution of your opponents' 5 cards is 3-2 and that both the Jack and the Ten will fall on the first 3 rounds.

If one of your opponents plays the Jack or the Ten on the first round, the other opponent probably holds the other honor, guarded. Plan to finesse against it.

⑦ K Q 9 6 5 ♣ ♣ ♣ ♣ ♣

A 10 3 2 ♣ ♣ ♣ ♣

⑧ K Q 9 6 ♦ ♦ ♦ ♦

A 8 3 2 ♦ ♦ ♦ ♦

THE POSTPONED FINESSE

When you finesse against the King, there is a 50% chance that it is on the wrong side and that your finesse will fail.

There is also a chance that the King is a singleton and will drop if you play your Ace on the first round. If the King does not drop, you can still lead up to your Queen and finesse it against the King on the second round of the suit.

The chances that the King is a singleton on the wrong side are as follows:

Opponents Hold	King is Singleton	Singleton on Wrong Side
2 cards	52% of the time	26% of the time
3 cards	26% of the time	13% of the time
4 cards	13% of the time	6% of the time
5 cards	6% of the time	3% of the time
6 cards	3% of the time	1½% of the time

When your Ace and Queen are in the same hand, do not try to drop the King unless you and the dummy hold 11 cards, and there are only 2 cards out against you. Finesse your Queen on the first round.

When your Ace and Queen are divided between your hand and the dummy, as in Examples 1, 2, and 3, you can increase your chances of taking a trick with your Queen if you play your Ace on the first round and try to drop a singleton King.

Nevertheless, finesse your Queen on the first round if you will need your Ace as a stopper or as an entry after you have tried the finesse. The remote chance of dropping a singleton King held over your Queen is not worth the high cost of using for that purpose a stopper or entry you need.

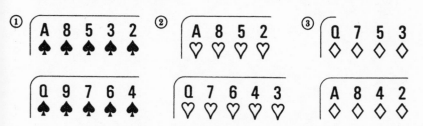

Your Ace will drop a singleton King held over your Queen 13% of the time in Example 1, 6% in Example 2, and 3% in Example 3.

When you finesse against the Queen, your chances of finding it a singleton are the same as your chances of finding a singleton King.

Nevertheless, even though the chance that you will drop a singleton Queen held on the wrong side is very small, there is usually no harm in trying. Play your Ace on the first round and postpone your finesse until the second round.

Do not postpone your finesse, however, under the following conditions:

a. You have no way to reenter the hand from which you must lead to finesse against the Queen, or your only entry to that hand is one that you might need for another purpose, as might be the case in Example 4.

b. You hold the Ace and King in 1 hand and the Ten, Nine, and Eight in the other, as in Example 5. In case West holds both the Queen and Jack with one or more low cards, you will need both your Ace and King to capture West's Queen and Jack when you finesse against them.

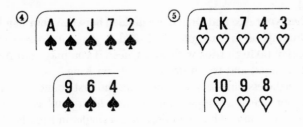

When you finesse against the Jack, postpone your finesse as long as possible if you hold the 3 top honors, as in Examples 6, 7, and 8. The Jack may fall and the finesse become unnecessary.

In Example 6 play out your Ace and King before you finesse against the Jack. There is an 18% chance that the Jack will drop if you postpone your finesse until the third round.

In Example 7 the second round is your last chance to lead from South for a finesse. Your chance of finding the Jack a singleton on the wrong side is only $\frac{1}{2}$ of 1%, but you have nothing to lose by postponing your finesse.

In Example 8 your only chance to finesse is on the first round.

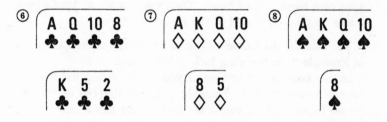

Of course, do not postpone your finesse if you have no way to reenter the hand from which you must lead for a finesse, or if your only entry is one that you might need for another purpose.

THE DOUBLE FINESSE

A double finesse consists of 2 finesses you make in the same suit when your opponents hold 2 honors against which you must finesse.

WHEN YOUR HONORS ARE HELD IN THE SAME HAND

The 2 cards you finesse may be equal honors, like the Jack-Ten in Example 1.

In that case on the first round you finesse one of your 2 equal honors. It will either take the trick or drive out 1 of your opponents' 2 higher honors and establish a simple finessing position for your own second equal honor. Then you can finesse your second honor on the next round of the suit.

The 2 cards you finesse may form a tenace, like the Queen-Ten in Example 2, or the King-Jack in Example 3.

In that case, on the first round you usually finesse the lower of your 2 tenace cards. In Example 2, finesse the Ten on the first round. In Example 3, finesse the Jack on the first round.

① A J 10 5 ♡ ♡ ♡ ♡   ② A Q 10 ◇ ◇ ◇   ③ K J 7 ♡ ♡ ♡

8 4 3 ♡ ♡ ♡   8 7 6 ◇ ◇ ◇   8 6 4 ♡ ♡ ♡

The odds are as follows:

52% of the time, when the 2 adverse honors are divided, the first card you finesse will be captured, while the second card you finesse will take a trick.

24% of the time, when both adverse honors are favorably located for you, both cards you finesse will take tricks.

24% of the time, when both adverse cards are unfavorably located for you, neither card you finesse will take a trick.

WHEN YOUR HONORS ARE DIVIDED BETWEEN 2 HANDS

When your honors are divided between your hand and the dummy, do not lead an honor for a direct finesse, unless you can lead 1 of 3 equal cards, such as the Jack-Ten-Nine, or the Ten-Nine-Eight, as in Examples 4, 5, and 6.

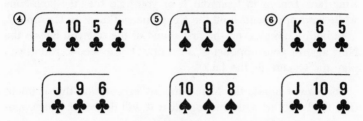

CHOOSING BETWEEN A SINGLE AND A DOUBLE FINESSE

Occasionally, when you hold a double finesse position, you should make a single finesse on the first round of the suit by finessing the highest of your tenace cards.

The number of cards you hold in the suit usually determines whether you should try a double or a single finesse.

When, as in Examples 7 and 9, you hold 8 cards or fewer, choose a double finesse. In Example 7, finesse the Ten on the first round. In Example 9, finesse the Jack.

When, as in Example 8, you hold 9 cards or more headed by Ace-Queen-Ten, choose a single finesse. In Example 8, finesse the Queen on the first round.

The general rule is: Eight or Less—Double Finesse.

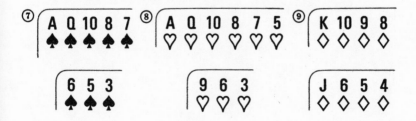

THE TRIPLE FINESSE

You make a triple finesse, or a deep finesse, when you finesse against 3 outstanding honors.

The opportunity to make a triple finesse comes when in 1 hand you hold the Ace-Queen-Nine, while your opponents hold the King-Jack-Ten, as in Example 1; or you hold the Ace-Jack-Nine while your opponents hold the King-Queen-Ten, as in Example 2.

In both Examples, on the first round of the suit you finesse the Nine against your opponents' 3 honors. On the second round you play the Queen (or the Jack).

You do not finesse the Nine with any expectation that it might take the trick but with the hope that it will drive out your opponents' King or Queen.

This triple finesse improves greatly your chances of taking a trick with your Queen or Jack.

In Example 1, if you finesse your Queen on the first round, it will take a trick 50% of the time. If you finesse the Nine on the first round, your Queen will take a trick 63% of the time.

In Example 2, if you finesse your Jack on the first round, it will take a trick 24% of the time. If you finesse the Nine on the first round, your Jack will take a trick 35% of the time.

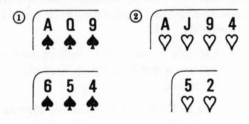

THE BACKWARD FINESSE

When you and the dummy hold all the honors in a suit except the Queen, with the Ace in 1 hand and the King in the other, as in Example 1, you are able to finesse against the Queen in either direction you choose.

Usually you would play the high card in the short hand first and then lead up to the tenace in the long hand for a finesse.

But sometimes you should make a backward finesse; that is, you should finesse in the opposite direction.

In Example 1 you make a backward finesse if you lead the Jack of Clubs for a direct finesse against the Queen.

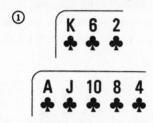

1. You should make a backward finesse whenever something in the bidding or in the previous play makes you think that a finesse in the normal direction will not succeed.
2. You should make a backward finesse whenever you cannot afford to lose the lead to the opponent who sits behind a tenace you hold in the long hand, as in Example 2.

CONTRACT
   3 Notrump
OPENING LEAD
   K of Spades

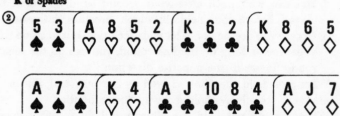

Hold up your Ace until the third round of Spades. Then West most probably has 2 Spades left and East none. If West regains the lead, he can set the contract.

You cannot afford to risk a finesse against the Queen of Clubs in the usual direction. Make a backward finesse by leading the Jack of Clubs for a direct finesse.

Even if East holds the Queen and takes the trick, he cannot then lead back a Spade.

THE 2-WAY FINESSE

When you and the dummy hold all the honors in a suit except the Queen, with the Ace in one hand and the King in the other, you can finesse in either direction you choose.

If you have no idea where the Queen is, try a 2-way finesse.

You make a 2-way finesse when, as in Examples 1 and 2, you lead the Jack (or its equal) from the South hand, as you would for a direct finesse against the Queen. You hope that if West holds the Queen, he will cover your Jack.

If, however, West plays low, you usually go up with your Ace (or King) in the North hand. Then you lead from North for a finesse against the Queen in the opposite direction, i.e., through the East hand. If, however, when West plays low you suspect that he holds the Queen, let your Jack ride for a direct finesse against West.

① A J 5 ♠ ♠ ♠   ② A 5 2 ♣ ♣ ♣   ③ K 10 4 ◇ ◇ ◇

K 10 9 ♠ ♠ ♠   K J 10 ♣ ♣ ♣   A J 5 ◇ ◇ ◇

You hold a 2-way finesse position against the Queen when you are able to do all of the following things:

1. You can start a direct finesse by leading the Jack or its equal in order to coax out the Queen.
2. You can wait until after your second hand opponent has played, before you decide in which direction to finesse.
3. In case you decide not to let your Jack ride, but to go up with your Ace or King on the first round, you can on the second round finesse in the opposite direction.

When you hold the Nine as well as the Jack and Ten, as in Example 1, you always hold a 2-way finesse position.

When you do not hold the Nine, you hold a 2-way finesse position only if your Jack and Ten are in the same hand as in Example 2.

In Example 3 you do not hold a 2-way finesse position.

THE FREE FINESSE

Any finesse that does not cost you a trick if it fails is a free finesse.

For instance—In Example 1 your opponent leads the Jack of Diamonds. Dummy holds the Ace and Queen, and you are blank in Diamonds.

If you finesse your Queen, you cannot lose a trick, because you can trump the trick if East covers the Queen with the King.

If, however, your Queen wins the trick, you can discard a losing Spade.

CONTRACT
  4 Hearts
OPENING LEAD
  J of Diamonds

Sometimes an opportunity to make a free finesse is not as obvious. In Example 2 your opponent leads the 5 of Hearts. Dummy holds the Ace and Queen and you hold a singleton Heart.

Your only chance to make the contract is to finesse the Queen of Hearts. If the Queen wins, you will be able to discard your losing Club on the Ace of Hearts.

If the finesse fails you will be set 1 trick. But the finesse has not cost you a trick. If you do not take the finesse, you are sure to go down 1 trick, because the only way you can get rid of your losing Club is to discard it on the Ace of Hearts.

CONTRACT
  6 Spades
OPENING LEAD
  5 of Hearts

THE TRUMP FINESSE

When you are playing a trump contract, and in 1 hand you hold a sequence of honors in a side suit, such as the King-Queen or the Queen-Jack-Ten, and in the other hand you are void in the suit, as in Examples 1 and 2, you have an opportunity to make a very useful kind of direct finesse, called a trump finesse.

Lead out your top honor. If it is covered by the next player, trump the trick. If it is not covered, discard a loser you hold in some other suit.

When you make a trump finesse against the Ace alone, as in Example 1, the King-Queen is a sufficient sequence of honors.

When you make a trump finesse against both the Ace and King, as in Example 2, you must hold 3 honors, the Queen-Jack-Ten.

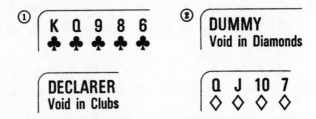

The trump finesse is always profitable to some extent, even when the honor you lead is not covered by the second player and is captured by the fourth.

In that event, although you have lost the trick, you have discarded a loser, and at the same time you have either established a winner, as in Example 1, or you have helped to establish a winner, as in Example 2.

THE OBLIGATORY FINESSE

Sometimes you hold the King in one hand and the Queen in the other, but no other honors in either hand, as in Examples 1, 2, and 3.

If on the first round of the suit you lead up to the Queen, and it takes the trick, you may assume that West holds the Ace, and that your King cannot take a trick if you play it on the second round of the suit.

Consequently, on the second round when you lead back toward the King, duck and finesse a low card, no matter how deep the finesse must be. Do not play your King, even if East puts up the Jack.

You do not take the deep finesse with any hope that your low card will take the trick. You hope that West's Ace was the top of a doubleton, and that he will have to play his Ace on the second round.

When you lead back toward your King on the second round, if East follows suit the chances that West's Ace was the top of a doubleton are approximately as follows:

100% when, as in Example 1, your opponents were dealt 4 cards
 40% when, as in Example 2, your opponents were dealt 5 cards
 20% when, as in Example 3, your opponents were dealt 6 cards
 10% when your opponents were dealt 7 cards

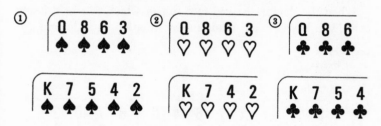

GET RID OF LOSERS

There are 4 ways you, the declarer, can get rid of losers you hold.

1. By ruffing them with dummy's otherwise worthless trumps.
2. By discarding them when winning cards are led from the dummy and you cannot follow suit.
3. By throwing a loser on a loser; that is, by discarding a loser you hold in another suit when you cannot follow suit on a trick that your opponents will take.
4. By making an end play.

RUFF WITH DUMMY'S TRUMPS

Small trumps in the dummy that will fall when trumps are led are useless unless, before you draw trumps, you can use them to ruff losing cards that you hold. They are called otherwise worthless trumps.

You cannot expect to be able to ruff a loser you hold in a suit when dummy holds more than 2 cards in that suit. One of your opponents will almost always be able to ruff before you can draw dummy's third card in the suit.

READY-MADE RUFFING POSITION

When the dummy is void in a suit in which you hold losing cards, you have a ready-made ruffing situation, as in Example 1.

CONTRACT
  4 Hearts
OPENING LEAD
  Q of Clubs

You can ruff all 3 of your losing Spades if you do so before you lead trumps.

DEVELOP RUFFING POSITION

Usually, however, in order to ruff with dummy's otherwise worthless trumps, you must develop a ruffing situation. When dummy holds a singleton or doubleton in a side suit in which you hold 1 or more losing cards, such as the Heart suit in Example 2, you can create a ruffing situation if you continue to lead that suit until dummy is void in it.

CONTRACT
   4 Spades
OPENING LEAD
   K of Diamonds

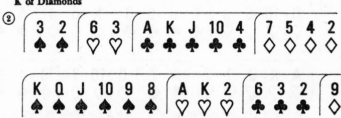

> Trump the second round of Diamonds. Then lead your Ace and King of Hearts to create a ruffing situation. Then ruff your losing Heart with 1 of dummy's otherwise worthless trumps.

If you have to give up the lead 1 or more times before you have removed all dummy's cards in his short suit, experienced opponents will try to keep you from establishing a ruffing situation by leading trumps every time they get the lead.

Consequently, you cannot expect to set up a ruffing position unless dummy holds enough trumps to follow suit each time your opponents lead a trump and still have a trump left with which to ruff your loser, as in Example 3.

CONTRACT
   4 Spades
OPENING LEAD
   9 of Diamonds

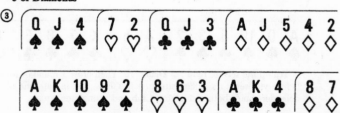

> If you are to make your contract, dummy must ruff 1 of your losing Hearts. You will have to lose the lead twice before dummy will be void in Hearts. Your opponents will lead trumps each time they get the lead. But dummy will still have 1 otherwise worthless trump with which to ruff your third Heart.

WHEN TO DRAW TRUMPS BEFORE RUFFING

Occasionally, the dummy holds enough trumps to let you draw all your opponents' trumps and still have a trump left to ruff your loser, as in Example 4. You can seldom draw all your **opponents' trumps before you ruff, unless the dummy holds 4 trumps.**

CONTRACT
4 Hearts
OPENING LEAD
9 of Spades

④

Q 10 5 3 ♡ ♡ ♡ ♡	K 8 5 3 ♣ ♣ ♣ ♣	K 6 4 ◇ ◇ ◇	A 7 ♠ ♠

A K J 7 2 ♡ ♡ ♡ ♡ ♡	A 7 ♣ ♣	Q 10 7 ◇ ◇ ◇	6 4 3 ♠ ♠ ♠

Unless 1 of your opponents holds all 4 of the outstanding trumps, you can afford to draw all your opponents' trumps before you start to set up a ruffing position.

Sometimes, even though you cannot afford to draw all your opponents' trumps before you start to develop a ruffing position, you can afford to draw 1 or 2 rounds, as in Example 5. **It is wise to draw all the trumps you can afford to, in order to reduce the chances of an unexpected ruff or overruff by one of your opponents.**

CONTRACT
4 Spades
OPENING LEAD
Q of Diamonds

⑤

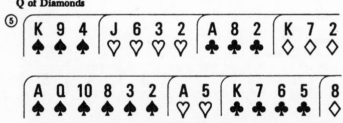

K 9 4 ♠ ♠ ♠	J 6 3 2 ♡ ♡ ♡ ♡	A 8 2 ♣ ♣ ♣	K 7 2 ◇ ◇ ◇

A Q 10 8 3 2 ♠ ♠ ♠ ♠ ♠ ♠	A 5 ♡ ♡	K 7 6 5 ♣ ♣ ♣ ♣	8 ◇

Trump the second round of Diamonds. Then draw 1 round of trumps before you set up a ruffing situation in Clubs, just in case one of the defenders holds both a singleton Club and a singleton trump.

In Examples 1, 2, and 3, on pages 30 and 31, you cannot afford to draw even 1 round of trumps before you ruff your losers.

RUFF TO ESTABLISH DECLARER'S SIDE SUIT

Sometimes, as in Example 6, in order to make your contract, you must take a trick with a low card in a long side suit you hold. When you do not have enough high cards in that suit to clear it, you may be able to use dummy's trumps to ruff a round or two of the suit and thus help establish your low card winner.

CONTRACT
6 Spades
OPENING LEAD
K of Diamonds

In order to establish a low Heart as a winner without giving the defenders a Heart trick, ruff 2 of your 3 small Hearts with dummy's 2 trumps before you lead trumps.

WHEN TO RUFF HIGH

Frequently when you try to establish a low card winner in your side suit by ruffing, one of your opponents will be able to trump the suit as soon as the dummy can. In that event you must ruff with a high trump in the dummy to avoid an overruff, as in Example 7.

CONTRACT
4 Spades
OPENING LEAD
K of Clubs

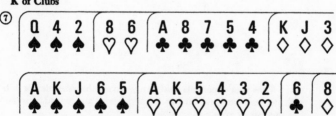

You must establish a low Heart as a winner without allowing your opponents to take a single Heart trick. Since your opponents hold 5 hearts, 1 of them is sure to hold no more than 2. Therefore, when you trump the third round of Hearts, trump with the Queen. If you trump with a low Spade, you may be overruffed by East.

You may be able to anticipate that an opponent will be able to overruff the dummy by the bidding or by the previous play. But if you have been given no information in this way, be guided by the probable distribution of the cards your opponents hold.*

DON'T RUFF WITH HIGH TRUMP YOU NEED TO DRAW OPPONENTS' TRUMPS

You win extra tricks when you ruff your losers with dummy's otherwise worthless trumps, even when those trumps are high cards such as the Queen in Example 7 on page 33.

But you do not gain a trick when you ruff with a high trump that you need in order to draw all your opponents' trumps, such as the Queen in Example 8.

CONTRACT
  4 Spades
OPENING LEAD
  K of Clubs

You must set up a low Heart as a winner. If on the third round of Hearts you trump low, you may be overruffed. Nevertheless, you cannot afford to trump with the Queen. You need it to keep your opponents from cashing 1 of their Spades.

*When your opponents hold an uneven number of cards in a suit: The chances are usually about 2 to 1 that the cards are divided between your opponents as evenly as possible.

When your opponents hold an even number of cards in a suit: The chances are usually about 2 to 1 that their cards are not evenly divided. One opponent usually holds 2 more cards than the other. See the table on page 3.

POSTPONE DRAWING TRUMPS

If you cannot draw your opponents' trumps without losing the lead, you must postpone leading trumps in situations such as the following.

1. **When you do not hold the top card in the suit from which you plan to discard your losers on dummy's winners,** as in Example 1, do not lead trumps until after you have discarded your losers.

CONTRACT
6 Hearts
OPENING LEAD
K of Spades

①
| K 7 | 8 6 3 | A K Q 5 | A K 5 3 |
| ♡ ♡ | ♣ ♠ ♠ | ♢ ♢ ♢ ♢ | ♣ ♣ ♣ ♣ |

| Q J 10 8 5 3 | A 9 4 | 6 | Q 4 2 |
| ♡ ♡ ♡ ♡ ♡ ♡ | ♠ ♠ ♠ | ♢ | ♣ ♣ ♣ |

Take the first trick with your Ace of Spades. Before you lead trumps, play your 3 top Diamonds. Discard your 2 losing Spades on the King and Queen of Diamonds.

2. **When the dummy's high cards must be promoted to become winners before you can discard your losers on them,** as in Example 2, do not lead trumps until after you have established dummy's high cards even though you hold the top card in the suit from which you plan to discard losers.

CONTRACT
4 Hearts
OPENING LEAD
Q of Clubs

②

| K 7 | A 6 3 | K Q J 4 | 10 9 6 4 |
| ♡ ♡ | ♣ ♠ ♠ | ♢ ♢ ♢ ♢ | ♣ ♣ ♣ ♣ |

| Q J 10 8 5 3 | 10 9 4 | 9 2 | A K |
| ♡ ♡ ♡ ♡ ♡ ♡ | ♠ ♠ ♠ | ♢ ♢ | ♣ ♣ |

Take the first trick with the Ace of Clubs. Before you lead trumps, lead a Diamond to establish your King and Queen of Diamonds as winners. If you lead trumps first, your opponents will capture the lead and force out your Ace of Spades. Then later, when they regain the lead with the Ace of Diamonds, they will take 2 Spade tricks before you can discard your 2 losing Spades on the Queen and Jack of Diamonds.

DISCARD LOSERS ON DUMMY'S WINNERS

When, as in Example 1, you can lead a winning card from the dummy, to which you cannot follow suit from your own hand, you can discard a loser on the trick.

CONTRACT
   6 Hearts
OPENING LEAD
   K of Spades

①

| K 7 | 8 6 3 | A K Q 5 | A K 5 3 |
| ♡ ♡ | ♠ ♠ ♠ | ◇ ◇ ◇ ◇ | ♣ ♣ ♣ ♣ |

| A Q J 8 5 3 | A 9 4 | 6 | 7 4 2 |
| ♡ ♡ ♡ ♡ ♡ ♡ | ♠ ♠ ♠ | ◇ | ♣ ♣ ♣ |

Win the first trick with the Ace of Spades. Draw trumps. Then play the Ace, King, and Queen of Diamonds. Discard your 2 losing Spades on the King and Queen of Diamonds.

USE DECLARER'S TRUMPS TO ESTABLISH DUMMY'S WINNERS

As a general rule, you should not ruff dummy's losers with your own small trumps except when you use them as stoppers or entries, or when you use them to help establish low cards in a long side suit in the dummy on which you can discard your own losers, as in Example 2.

CONTRACT
   4 Hearts
OPENING LEAD
   K of Spades

②

| Q J 6 4 | A 7 3 | 8 | A K 8 4 3 |
| ♡ ♡ ♡ ♡ | ♠ ♠ ♠ | ◇ | ♣ ♣ ♣ ♣ ♣ |

| A K 9 3 2 | 9 6 2 | A 10 2 | 6 5 |
| ♡ ♡ ♡ ♡ ♡ | ♠ ♠ ♠ | ◇ ◇ ◇ | ♣ ♣ |

Take the first trick with your Ace of Spades. Then take 2 trump tricks with your Ace and Queen. Then lead the Ace and King of Clubs and trump a third round of Clubs. If your opponents' Clubs are divided 3-3, you will have 2 low Club winners in the dummy on which you can discard your 2 losing Spades after you have drawn all your opponents' trumps.

THROW A LOSER ON A LOSER

When you hold a loser that you cannot ruff or discard on a winner in the opposite hand, sometimes it is best to throw the loser on a loser—that is, to discard it on a trick you let your opponents win in another suit even though you are void in that suit and could trump the trick.

It is profitable to throw a loser on a loser in situations such as the following.

1. **Declarer throws a loser on a loser because he cannot afford to trump.**

This situation occurs most often when you and the dummy hold 7 trumps divided 4-3, as in Example 1, and your opponents lead a long suit in which you are blank.

The odds are about 2 to 1 that the 6 trumps your opponents hold are not divided 3-3, and that one of your opponents holds at least 4 trumps.

In that event, if you trump the trick, one of your opponents will hold more trumps than you do. Then, after all your trumps are gone, he will be able to regain the lead by ruffing. Your opponents will then cash established cards in their long suit.

If, on the other hand, you discard a sure loser instead of trumping, you maintain your control of the trump suit.

Although you lose the immediate trick, this play does not cost you a trick in the long run, because, if you ruff and win the trick, you will lose a trick later when you have to follow suit with your loser.

CONTRACT
4 Spades
OPENING LEAD
K of Hearts

West takes the first 2 tricks with the Ace and King of Hearts and then leads the Queen of Hearts. If you ruff this trick, the odds are 2 to 1 that one of your opponents will end up with the last trump. In that case he will regain the lead and set the contract by cashing another Heart. Instead of ruffing the third trick, discard a Club.

2. **Declarer throws a loser on a loser to establish a winner in the dummy in situations such as the following.**

First: You are void in a suit in which dummy holds the second highest card outstanding. Your right hand opponent, East, leads a low card in that suit.

Do not trump. Instead, discard a sure loser you hold in another suit. West will have to play his top card on the trick. This will establish dummy's high card as a winner, on which you can later discard another loser. See Example 2.

CONTRACT
  2 Hearts
OPENING LEAD
  3 of Spades

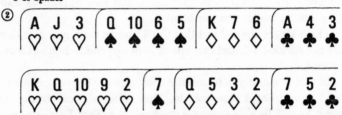

East takes the first trick with the Ace of Spades and returns a Spade. Do not trump. Discard 1 of your 2 losing Clubs instead. West has to play his King of Spades and your Queen of Spades becomes a winner. As soon as you get the lead, draw all your opponents' trumps. Then discard your second Club loser on the Queen of Spades.

Second: You make a trump finesse and throw a loser on a loser if the honor you lead is not covered, as in Example 3.

CONTRACT
  4 Spades
OPENING LEAD
  K of Diamonds

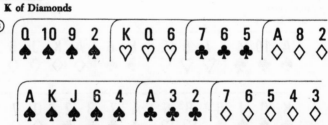

Take the first trick with dummy's Ace of Diamonds. Then lead dummy's King of Hearts. If East plays low, do not trump. Discard a losing Club. You will lose only 2 Diamond tricks and 1 Heart trick because you can discard your second Club loser on the Queen of Hearts and trump 2 of your losing Diamonds with the Queen and Ten of Spades.

3. **Dummy throws a loser on a loser to avoid an overruff and thereby sets up a ruffing position in another suit in the dummy.**

This situation is encountered when your opponent leads a winner in a suit that the dummy can trump; however, dummy cannot win the trick because he will be overruffed.

Occasionally, when this is the case, it is profitable for dummy to throw a loser he holds in another suit to develop a ruffing position that will allow him later to ruff a loser that declarer holds in that suit.

Example 4 illustrates this situation.

CONTRACT
  4 Hearts
OPENING LEAD
  K of Clubs

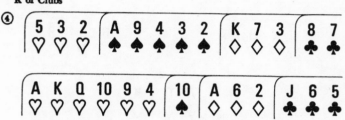

West leads the King of Clubs, then the Queen. East follows with a high card on the first trick, then a low card on the second, urging his partner to lead the suit again. Obviously he has no more Clubs and can overruff if dummy trumps the third round.

If, however, you let West win the trick and throw one of dummy's 2 low Diamonds, you will establish a ruffing situation in the dummy's Diamond suit which will enable you to trump one of your own losing Diamonds with one of dummy's low trumps.

THE END PLAY

An end play, or throw-in play, usually occurs on the third or fourth trick from the end of the hand.

You make an end play when you lead a card that forces a particular opponent to take the trick, and that opponent will then have to lead a card that will give you a trick that you could not, or might not, otherwise take if you had to lead that suit.

Sometimes, when you have end-played an opponent, he must give you a trick by leading up to a finesse position you hold, as in Examples 1 and 2.

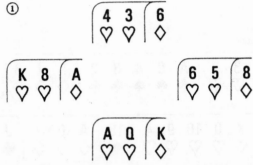

You need 2 of the last 3 tricks to make your contract. Dummy has the lead. If you lead a Heart and finesse your Queen, you have a 50% chance to make your contract. If, however, you lead a Diamond, West will be forced to take the trick and lead back a Heart. Then your Ace and Queen will each take a trick, no matter where the King is.

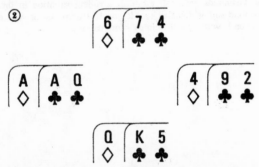

You must take a trick with the King of Clubs to make your contract. Dummy has the lead. Do not risk a finesse. Lead a Diamond. Then your King is sure to take a trick, no matter who holds the Ace.

Sometimes, when you are playing a trump contract and have end-played your opponent, he must give you a ruff and a sluff by leading a suit that you can ruff in one hand while you discard from the other hand a sure loser in another suit, as in Example 3.

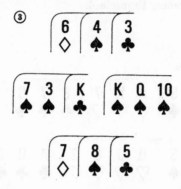

Example 3. Diamonds are trumps. If you lead a Spade, East will take the trick and will be forced to return a Spade. Then you can ruff in one hand and discard a losing Club from the other. Each of your 2 trumps will take a trick.

The average player seldom recognizes that he has an opportunity to make an end play until the third or fourth trick from the end of the hand. Then he realizes that he has unintentionally developed an end play situation in which he can make an opponent lead up to a finesse position in the dummy or in his own hand, as in Examples 1 and 2, or give him a ruff and a sluff, as in Example 3.

The expert, however, can usually recognize early in the play of the hand that he has an opportunity to create a situation in which he can use an end play.

When he does, he develops the end play position by leading out his high cards in the suits he does not want led at the end, and removing from his opponents' hands all the cards they hold in these suits.

Meanwhile, the expert saves a low card in his own hand or in the dummy with which he can force an opponent to take the trick when that opponent will have to lead back the suit that will assure the expert of a trick he might not otherwise make.

Take, for instance, Example 4.

CONTRACT
  6 Notrump
OPENING LEAD
  J of Diamonds

④
| K J 9 ♠ ♠ ♠ | A K 7 ♡ ♡ ♡ | 8 7 6 ♣ ♣ ♣ | A Q 7 4 ◇ ◇ ◇ ◇ |

| A Q 3 ♠ ♠ ♠ | Q J 6 2 ♡ ♡ ♡ ♡ | A Q 5 ♣ ♣ ♣ | K 6 5 ◇ ◇ ◇ |

You have 11 sure tricks, 1 sure loser (the 5 of Clubs) and 1 potential loser (the Queen of Clubs). The average player would try to develop his twelfth trick first by establishing a low card Diamond winner. In case his opponents' Diamonds did not break 3-3, he would then try to finesse the Queen of Clubs.

The expert player would start out the same way. If East showed out of Diamonds on the second or third round, he would know that West's Ten would control the fourth round of Diamonds.

Before risking a Club finesse, the expert would try to develop the end play position shown in Example 5 with the lead in the dummy. Then, by leading a Diamond he would force West to take the trick and lead back a Club to his Ace-Queen.

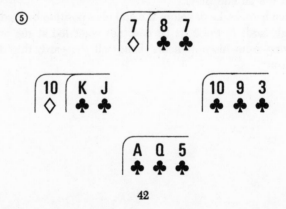

⑤

As soon as East shows out of Diamonds, the expert leads out all his high Spades, Hearts, and Diamonds, and in so doing he strips West's hand of all Hearts and Spades, leaving him only Clubs and Diamonds. He has saved dummy's last Diamond to force West to take the eleventh trick. West must lead back a Club, and both the Ace and Queen of Clubs will win, no matter who holds the King.

Example 6 shows the complete deal.

(6)

```
                         NORTH
                    K♠  A♥  8♣  A♦
                    J♠  K♥  7♣  Q♦
                    9♠  3♥  6♣  7♦
                                4♦

   WEST                                      EAST
  5♠ 4♠ 2♠                                    3♦
  9♥ 4♥                                   2♣ 3♣ 9♣ 10♣
  K♣ J♣ 4♣                                5♥ 7♥ 8♥ 10♥
  J♦ 10♦ 9♦ 8♦ 2♦                         6♠ 7♠ 8♠ 10♠

                         SOUTH
                    A  Q  3
                    ♠  ♠  ♠
                    Q  J  6  2
                    ♥  ♥  ♥  ♥
                    A  Q  5
                    ♣  ♣  ♣
                    K  6  5
                    ♦  ♦  ♦
```

ENTRIES AND STOPPERS

ENTRIES

An entry is a card that will take a trick when you lead up to it from the opposite hand. An entry allows you to shift the lead from one hand to the other.

OBVIOUS ENTRIES

A card that is higher than any card that the opponents hold in that suit is an obvious entry, provided you hold a smaller card in the opposite hand that you can lead up to it.

In Example 1 the following cards are obvious entries: Ace, King, and Queen of Hearts; Ace of Clubs; either the Ace or King of Diamonds, but not both. Dummy's second Diamond is not an entry, because you cannot lead up to it from the opposite hand.

CONTRACT

4 Spades

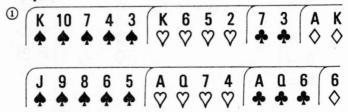

POTENTIAL ENTRIES

1. A card that might win as a result of a successful finesse is a potential entry.
2. A card that might eventually be promoted to top rank, while you still have a lower card in the opposite hand to lead up to it, is a potential entry.

In Example 1 the following cards are potential entries: King of Spades; Seven of Hearts; Queen of Clubs.

HIDDEN ENTRIES

A card that might eventually be promoted to top rank, if in the opposite hand you can get rid of a higher card and keep a lower card to lead up to the promoted card is a hidden entry.

Hidden entries most often occur when each partner holds 4 cards in the same suit.

In Example 1 the Six of Hearts is a hidden entry provided you play your Seven of Hearts when you lead up to the King and save your Four of Hearts to lead up to the Six on the fourth round of the suit.

RUFFING ENTRIES

A ruffing entry is any trump with which you can ruff without being overruffed when a suit in which you are void is led from the opposite hand.

Occasionally the only way to cross over to the other hand is to ruff the top card in the suit, even the Ace.

In Example 2 a small trump can be used as a ruffing entry by trumping the Ace or King of Hearts.

CONTRACT
4 Spades

② 5 4 3 2 ♠ ♠ ♠ ♠ | 2 ♡ | 8 7 6 5 4 ♣ ♣ ♣ ♣ ♣ | J 10 9 ◇ ◇ ◇

A K Q J 6 ♠ ♠ ♠ ♠ ♠ | A K ♡ ♡ | J 10 3 ♣ ♣ ♣ | A Q 8 ◇ ◇ ◇

THE USE OF ENTRIES

There are many occasions when you need an entry to shift the lead from one hand to the other. Those that arise most frequently are the following.

1. You want to enter the opposite hand in order to lead up to a high card or a tenace in your own hand.

In Example 2 you want to enter the dummy in order to lead the Jack of Diamonds for a direct finesse to capture the King.

2. You want to enter a hand in order to cash the cards remaining in a suit after they have been established as winners.

In Example 3 you want to enter the dummy, after you have played your Ace and King of Diamonds, in order to cash dummy's remaining Diamonds.

CONTRACT
6 Notrump
OPENING LEAD
J of Hearts

③ K J 2 ♠ ♠ ♠ | 5 4 2 ♡ ♡ ♡ | 8 ♣ | Q J 10 5 4 2 ◇ ◇ ◇ ◇ ◇ ◇

Q 8 ♠ ♠ | A K Q ♡ ♡ ♡ | A K 7 5 4 2 ♣ ♣ ♣ ♣ ♣ ♣ | A K ◇ ◇

CONSERVE YOUR ENTRIES

Whenever you need a high card you hold as an entry, such as the Ace and King of Clubs in Example 4, do not play it prematurely unless you are forced to do so.

Whenever you are able to take a trick in either hand, stop and consider carefully which card you should choose to win the trick. Do not take the trick with a card you will need later for an entry.

CONTRACT
   3 Notrump
OPENING LEAD
   J of Spades

④

| ♠ 6 3 | ♡ 7 6 4 | ♣ A K 3 2 | ◇ 10 9 8 3 |

| ♠ A K 2 | ♡ A Q | ♣ Q 6 5 4 | ◇ A Q 4 2 |

Do not run your Club suit until after you have established your Diamond suit. Use your Ace and King of Clubs as entries to the dummy in order to make 2 Diamond finesses.

STOPPERS

A stopper is a card that will win a trick in your opponents' strong suit and prevent them from running it without interruption.

Aces and adequately guarded honors serve as stoppers as well as entries. A trump is a stopper for a suit in which you are void.

Conserve your stoppers as long as you can. Play them only to stop your opponents from running their strong suit, or when you must use them as entries and no other card will do. Do not play them, if you can avoid it, until you have developed all the tricks you need in other suits.

Examples are given on page 81.

DUCKING

You duck if you play a low card instead of a high one when your high card would, or might, win the trick.

DUCK TO ESTABLISH
DUMMY'S LONG SUIT

When the dummy has a long suit that you must establish, but there are no entries to the dummy outside that suit, and not enough high cards in the suit to run it without interruption, you must duck on the first round of the suit.

In Example 1 duck on the first round of Clubs instead of playing your Ace or King.

CONTRACT
  3 Notrump
OPENING LEAD
  4 of Hearts

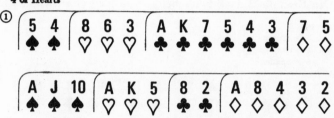

If you play dummy's Ace or King of Clubs on the first round of the suit, you will take only 2 Club tricks. Your opponents are sure to win the third round of Clubs. You will be unable to enter the dummy again to cash your 3 remaining Clubs.

Therefore, duck—play low from the dummy—on the first round of Clubs, and play your Ace and King on the second and third rounds. There is a 68% chance that your opponents' Clubs are divided 3-2. When they are, all of them will fall on the first 3 rounds of the suit, and you will take 5 Club tricks.

In Example 2 duck on the first round of the Heart suit and finesse your Queen on the second round.

CONTRACT
   3 Notrump
OPENING LEAD
   9 of Spades

To make your contract you need 5 Heart tricks. Your best chance is to find your opponents' Hearts divided 3-2 with the King in West's hand.
   There is a 37% chance that this will be the case. So duck on the first round of Hearts and finesse your Queen on the second round.

In Example 3 duck twice before you play your Ace of Clubs.

CONTRACT
   3 Notrump
OPENING LEAD
   J of Spades

③ | 7 2 | 6 4 3 | A 8 7 5 4 | 8 6 5 |
    | ♠ ♠ | ♡ ♡ ♡ | ♣ ♣ ♣ ♣ ♣ | ♢ ♢ ♢ |

    | A K Q 6 | K Q 8 | 9 3 2 | A K 4 |
    | ♠ ♠ ♠ ♠ | ♡ ♡ ♡ | ♣ ♣ ♣ | ♢ ♢ ♢ |

To make your contract you must take 3 Club tricks. Your only chance to do this is to duck the first two rounds of Clubs. Then enter the dummy with your Ace on the third round.
   There is a 68% chance that your opponents' Clubs will be divided 3-2. Whenever they are, you will cash your Ace and 2 small Clubs.

In Example 4 you must duck in order to establish dummy's long suit, even though the dummy holds an entry in another suit.

CONTRACT
   3 Notrump
OPENING LEAD
   J of Spades

To make your contract you must take 3 Club tricks. The only way you can hope to do this is to duck 2 rounds of Clubs before you play dummy's Ace of Clubs. Since you hold only 2 Clubs, dummy's Ace of Clubs must not be used as an entry. Save dummy's King of Diamonds to be used as an entry after 2 rounds of Clubs have been played. Then you can cash your Ace of Clubs and 2 small Clubs if your opponents' Clubs are divided 3-3. They will be so divided only 36% of the time. The odds are 2 to 1 against you, but it is the only chance you have to take 3 Club tricks.

THE HOLD-UP PLAY

The hold-up play is a ducking play. You hold up when you can stop a suit your opponents have led, but you let them take 1 or more tricks in that suit before you play your stopper.

HOLD UP WHEN PLAYING A NOTRUMP CONTRACT

You use the hold-up play most often when you are playing a Notrump contract and one of your opponents leads from a long suit—a suit that will set the contract if your opponents can establish it and run it.

When this is the case, hold up your stopper until one of your opponents will be unable to lead the suit again if he captures the lead.

If you are uncertain when that will be, hold up until the third round of the suit.

Then, after you have played your stopper, do your best to keep the lead away from the opponent who holds the remaining cards in the established suit.

When your stopper is the Ace and 2 small cards (Axx), as in the Heart suit in Example 1, hold up until the third round.

CONTRACT
   3 Notrump
OPENING LEAD
   4 of Hearts

West probably holds 5 Hearts and East 3. So hold up your Ace of Hearts until the third round. Then try to keep West from getting the lead. Lead your Ace of Diamonds and finesse against the Queen on the second round. If East holds the Queen and takes the trick, he cannot lead a Heart. You will take the next trick no matter which suit East leads. Then you can run your long Diamond suit and make your contract.

When your stopper consists of the King and Queen and 1 small card, the King and Queen may both be in the same hand, as in the Club suit in Example 2, or they may be divided between your own hand and the dummy, as in Example 3.

In either case, play your cards in such a way that you will be sure to stop the suit on the third round.

CONTRACT
   3 Notrump
OPENING LEAD
   5 of Clubs

② | K 5 ♠ ♠ | A 5 3 ♡ ♡ ♡ | 8 3 2 ♣ ♣ ♣ | A Q 9 8 3 ◇ ◇ ◇ ◇ ◇ |

| A 9 6 ♠ ♠ ♠ | K Q 7 ♡ ♡ ♡ | K Q 6 ♣ ♣ ♣ | J 10 4 2 ◇ ◇ ◇ ◇ |

East plays the Jack of Clubs on the first trick. If you take this trick with your Queen, you will be unable to stop the third round of Clubs. If East holds the King of Diamonds, he will get the lead when you try to set up your Diamonds. He will return a Club. Your King will be captured and your opponents will run their Club suit and set the contract.

If, however, you play low on the first trick, you are sure to stop the third round of Clubs. Then, if East gets the lead with his King of Diamonds, he will have no Clubs left. Your opponents cannot cash their good Clubs and you will make your contract.

CONTRACT
   3 Notrump
OPENING LEAD
   5 of Clubs

③ | K 5 4 ♠ ♠ ♠ | A 5 3 ♡ ♡ ♡ | Q 3 ♣ ♣ | A Q 9 8 3 ◇ ◇ ◇ ◇ ◇ |

| A 9 6 ♠ ♠ ♠ | K Q 7 ♡ ♡ ♡ | K 8 6 ♣ ♣ ♣ | J 10 4 2 ◇ ◇ ◇ ◇ |

Do not play either your Queen or King of Clubs on the first trick. If you play low, you are sure to stop the suit on the third round.

If, however, you play either one of your honors on the first trick, even when your honor wins the trick, your contract will be set if East holds the King of Diamonds. When East gets the lead, he will return a Club, and your opponents will run their long Club suit.

When your stopper is the King-Jack tenace (KJx), as in the Heart suit in Example 4, do not play your King until the third round of the suit.

CONTRACT
3 Notrump
OPENING LEAD
5 of Hearts

If East plays the Queen on the first round, do not take the trick with your King. If you do, you won't be able to stop the third round of Hearts.

If East plays the Ace on the first round and leads back a Heart, play your Jack, not your King. Save your King to stop the third round.

When your stopper is the King and 2 small cards (Kxx), as in the Heart suit in Example 5, hold up your King until the third round unless it will be captured if you do not play it on the first trick.

CONTRACT
3 Notrump
OPENING LEAD
5 of Hearts

If East plays the Ace on the first trick, you can safely hold up your King until the third round of the suit.

If East plays any card other than the Ace, your King will be captured unless you play it on the first trick. You cannot afford to hold up.

When your stopper is the Ace, Jack and 1 small card (Ajx), as in the Spade suit in Example 6, you can make a very effective kind of hold-up play called the Bath Coup.

When your opponents' opening lead is a King, which you recognize as a lead from a long suit headed by King-Queen, as in Example 6, hold up your Ace on the first round.

If West continues the suit, no matter whether his second lead is the Queen or a low card, both your Ace and Jack will take tricks.

If West shifts to another suit, you will have stopped his long suit once without playing your Ace. You will be able to stop it a second time by playing your Ace on either the second or third round of the suit, whichever you prefer.

If, however, you play your Ace to take the first trick, your opponents' long suit will be established immediately. If East gets the lead and returns the suit. Your opponents will then cash their remaining low cards in the suit.

CONTRACT
  3 Notrump
OPENING LEAD
  K of Spades

Let West's King of Spades take the trick. If West now leads a low Spade, your Jack will take the trick, and you will still have the Ace to stop the third round of Spades. If West's second lead is the Queen of Spades, your Ace will take the trick and your Jack will stop the third round.

If West shifts and leads any suit other than Spades on the second trick, play low from the dummy. Even when East holds both the King of Diamonds and the King of Clubs, you are sure to make your contract.

After East wins the second trick with one of his Kings and returns his partner's Spades, play your Jack, not your Ace, so you can stop the third round of Spades.

When East gets in again with his second King, he will have no Spade left to lead, so you can take the rest of your 9 tricks without interruption.

HOLD UP WITH DOUBLE STOPPER

Even when you hold both the Ace and King and 1 small card (AKx) of your opponents' long suit and can stop the suit twice, sometimes you should hold up on the first round. Duck whenever you might have to give up the lead twice before you can develop and take the 9 tricks you need to make your contract.

This first round hold-up prevents your opponents from establishing and running their long suit whenever the 2 cards to which you must give up the lead are divided between your opponents, and at the same time one of your opponents holds only 2 cards in their long suit.

In Example 7 suppose West holds the Ace of Clubs and 5 Hearts, while East holds the King of Clubs and 2 small Hearts.

CONTRACT
   3 Notrump
OPENING LEAD
   Q of Hearts

To make your contract you must establish and take 2 Club tricks. To do this, you must force your opponents to play both their Ace and King of Clubs before they can establish and run their long Heart suit.

If you play low and let West's Queen of Hearts win the first trick, West will lead the Jack of Hearts on the second trick, which you will win with your King of Hearts.

Now, when you lead to establish your Clubs, if East takes the trick with his King of Clubs, he cannot return his partner's Hearts. He leads another suit, and you regain the lead and lead another Club.

When West takes this trick with his Ace of Clubs, you still hold the Ace of Hearts to stop his long suit. So you regain the lead, cash your 2 good Clubs and make your contract.

All you need to remember is this general rule: **Whenever you might have to give up the lead twice before you can cash your 9 tricks, hold up on the first round even though you have a double stopper.**

DO NOT HOLD UP

1. It is not necessary to hold up when, without giving up the lead, you can immediately take all the tricks you need to make your contract, as in Example 1.

You may play your Ace of Diamonds on the first trick. You can take 9 sure tricks immediately without losing the lead—1 Diamond, 5 Clubs, 2 Hearts, and 1 Spade.

2. Do not hold up when the first trick may be your only chance to stop the suit, a now-or-never situation, as in Example 2.

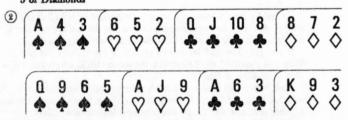

If East does not play the Ace, take the first trick with your King of Diamonds. This is your only chance to stop the Diamonds. If you let East take the first trick, he will return a Diamond, your King will be captured, and West will take 4 Diamond tricks.

Take the first trick with your King of Diamonds. Then enter the dummy with your Ace of Spades and lead the Queen of Clubs for a direct finesse against the King.

3. **Do not hold up when each of your opponents holds more cards in the suit than you hold,** as in Examples 3 and 4.

It is futile to hold up if both opponents can lead the suit after you have been forced to play your stopper.

CONTRACT
   3 Notrump
OPENING LEAD
   K of Hearts

③

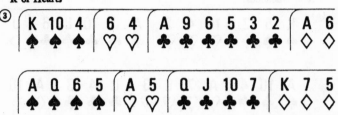

There is less than a 10% chance that one of your opponents holds only 1 or 2 Hearts. So both East and West hold more Hearts than you do. Do not hold up. You cannot keep East from leading a Heart if he gets in.

Take the first trick with your Ace of Hearts and try to establish your Clubs. If East holds the King of Clubs, you will go down at least 1 trick.

CONTRACT
   3 Notrump
OPENING LEAD
   2 of Hearts

④

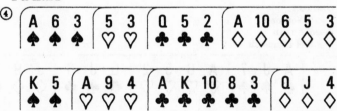

If West is leading his fourth best Heart, he holds only 4 Hearts, because there is no card lower than the 2. Therefore, since you and the dummy together hold 5 Hearts, East must hold 4 Hearts, the same number as West holds. Even if you hold up your Ace of Hearts until the third round, you cannot keep your opponents from taking a third Heart trick if either one of them secures the lead.

Therefore, play your Ace of Hearts on the first trick. Then, after you have run your Clubs, play your Ace and King of Spades. Then your Ace of Diamonds will give you your ninth trick.

4. **Do not hold up when by covering your opponent's honor on the first trick you will promote a card in your own hand or in the dummy which will become a second stopper and will win the third round of the suit, as in Examples 5 and 6.**

CONTRACT
    3 Notrump
OPENING LEAD
    9 of Diamonds

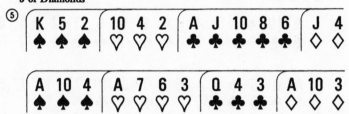

You play low from the dummy and East plays the Queen. Do not hold up. Cover the Queen with your Ace. Then lead your Queen of Clubs for a direct finesse against the King. If East wins the trick and leads his King of Diamonds, your Ten will stop the third round of Diamonds and your contract is assured.

If you hold up your Ace of Diamonds until the third round, you will take only 1 Diamond trick instead of 2. Then if East holds the King of Clubs, he will stop your Clubs and set your contract by cashing his good Diamonds.

CONTRACT
    1 Notrump
OPENING LEAD
    6 of Diamonds

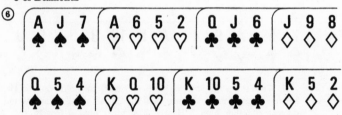

Play low from the dummy. East plays the Queen. If East held both the Queen and the Ten, he would have played the Ten instead of the Queen. So now you can be sure that West holds the Ten.

Cover East's Queen with your King. Now you can count on taking 2 Diamond tricks, because your Jack will stop the third round of the suit. Drive out the Ace of Clubs and you will make your contract.

5. **Do not hold up until one of your opponents has played his last card in his partner's long strong suit; that opponent will never be able to get the lead to return the suit.**

This is the situation when, as in Example 7, you hold the top card in each suit, and every finesse that you will have to take will be through the partner of the opponent who holds the long suit.

Of course, if any of your finesses should fail, your opponent will run his long suit. But this he will be able to do even if you hold up your stopper until the third round.

CONTRACT
3 Notrump
OPENING LEAD
K of Hearts

During the bidding West overcalled in Hearts. Do not hold up. Play your Ace. There is no need to exhaust East's hand of Hearts, because he can never get in to return his partner's Hearts.

To make your contract you must make a successful Club finesse. If East holds the King of Clubs, you have no problem. If, however, West holds the King of Clubs, your contract will be set even if you hold up your Ace of Hearts until the third round.

6. **Do not hold up when by so doing you give your opponents a chance to shift to another suit in which you are more vulnerable than in the suit that was led. Example 8.**

CONTRACT
2 Notrump
OPENING LEAD
5 of Spades

East plays the Ten of Spades. Do not hold up. You cannot afford to give East a chance to lead a Heart. Enter the dummy and lead the Queen of Diamonds for a direct finesse against the King. If East holds the King of Diamonds, you will make your contract.

HOLD UP WHEN PLAYING
A SUIT CONTRACT

When you are playing a trump contract, you can occasionally use the hold-up play to your advantage. But the purpose of the play at a trump contract is not the same as at Notrump. You do not use it to keep your opponents from running their long suit. Your trumps will prevent that.

The hold-up play at a trump contract is used for other reasons, among them the following.

1. **When you hold the AJx in a suit from which your opponent has led the King, sometimes you can use the Bath Coup effectively to keep your opponents from taking more than 1 trick in the suit.** See Example 1.

By holding up your Ace on the first round you force your opponent to switch to another suit. You stop his original suit without playing your Ace. You save your Ace to stop his suit when it is led a second time. In the meantime, you discard a loser in that suit from your hand or the dummy so you can trump the third round of the suit.

CONTRACT
  5 Clubs
OPENING LEAD
  K of Hearts

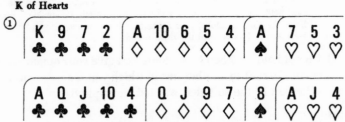

Do not take the first trick with your Ace of Hearts. If you do, and East holds the King of Diamonds, he will get the lead when you take your Diamond finesse. Then he will return his partner's Hearts, and you will lose 1 Diamond and 2 Heart tricks—down 1.

Hold up your Ace and let your opponent's King take the first trick. Then you are sure to make your contract.

If West's second lead is another Heart, you can take the trick and still have command of the suit in case East gets the lead with the King of Diamonds.

If West shifts to another suit, even if East gets in with the King of Diamonds, your Ace will stop the second round of Hearts. Then, after you have drawn trumps, you can discard your third Heart on dummy's fifth Diamond.

2. When you hold the Ace and 2 or 3 low cards in the suit your opponent has led, while the dummy holds a doubleton in that suit, as in Example 2, you want, if possible, to trump 1 or 2 of your low cards.

If you play your Ace on the first trick and then lead one of your low cards in the suit, your opponents will recognize what you plan to do. They will try to block your plan by leading trumps as soon as they take the second trick.

But if you hold up your Ace on the first trick, they may not realize that they should lead trumps immediately. They may lead the suit a second time, or switch to some other suit that will give you the lead.

Then after playing your Ace to draw dummy's last card in that suit, you can lead the suit again and trump 1 of your losing cards.

If, however, in your own hand you hold 4 cards in your opponent's suit, and the bidding has indicated that your other opponent may hold a singleton in that suit, play your Ace on the first round. If you hold it up until the second round, it might be trumped when you lead it.

CONTRACT
4 Hearts
OPENING LEAD
K of Spades

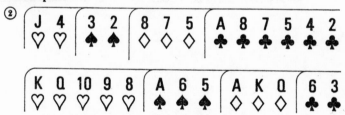

Hold up your Ace on the first trick. If West continues with another Spade, your Ace will take the trick. If he shifts to either Diamonds or Clubs, you will get the lead.

In either case, after you have played your Ace of Spades, you will be able to trump your last Spade before your opponents can draw dummy's trumps. In this way you can make your contract.

If, however, West's second lead is a trump and 2 rounds of trumps are played before you get in, dummy cannot ruff your last Spade. Your opponents will take 2 Spades, 1 Heart, and 1 Club trick to set your contract.

3. **When you hold the Ace in the suit that has been led, sometimes by refusing to take the first trick, you can keep the lead away from an opponent who could set the contract if he were to get in and lead another suit, against which you have no defense.** The Club suit in Example 3 is such a suit.

CONTRACT
  4 Spades
OPENING LEAD
  4 of Hearts

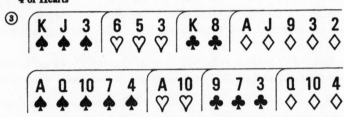

East plays the Queen of Hearts on the first trick. Play your Ten. If you take the first trick with your Ace, your contract can be set, if East holds both the Ace of Clubs and the King of Diamonds.

If West gets the lead again with the King or Jack of Hearts, he will lead a Club, and your opponents will take a total of 4 tricks: 1 Heart, 2 Clubs, and 1 Diamond.

This cannot happen if you hold up your Ace of Hearts on the first trick, because then West cannot regain the lead with a Heart. Your Ace will stop the second round of Hearts, and you can trump the third round.

PRELIMINARY ANALYSIS

Before planning how to play the hand, review the bidding and analyze the opening lead to look for any clues that might help you answer the following questions.

1. What is the distribution of the cards your opponents hold in any suit that is important to you and presents a problem?
2. What is the location of the honor cards your opponents hold?

If your opponents bid and lead in the conventional way that most good players do, clues may be found in any bids they have made and in the card that has been led.

CLUES TO DISTRIBUTION AVAILABLE FROM THE BIDDING

OPENING BID OF 1 IN A SUIT

An opening bid in a major suit indicates that the bidder holds at least 4 cards in that suit. He probably holds 5.

If he opened 1 Diamond, he probably holds either 4 or 5.

If he opened 1 Club, he is likely to hold only 3 Clubs; but he may hold 4 or 5 or more.

OPENING BID OF 3 IN A SUIT

The bidder usually holds at least 6 cards if the bid is in a major suit. If he bids a minor suit, he holds at least 6, probably 7.

OVERCALLS

An overcall in a suit indicates at least 5 cards in that suit.

A takeout double indicates 3 or 4 cards in each unbid suit.

REBIDS

When, on the first round of bidding an opponent has bid one suit, and on a later round has bid another that has not been mentioned before, he probably holds only 4 cards in his second suit.

When he rebids the suit he opened, before his partner has raised it, he usually holds at least 5 cards.

RESPONSES TO OPENING BID OF 1 IN A SUIT

A response of 1 Notrump indicates the responder does not hold 4 cards in a higher ranking suit, or in his partner's suit.

When he has raised his partner's suit, he usually holds at least 3 cards in that suit.

When he has bid 1 over 1, or 2 over 1, he usually holds at least 4 cards in his suit.

CLUES TO DISTRIBUTION AVAILABLE FROM THE OPENING LEAD

WHEN YOUR OPPONENT LEADS HIS PARTNER'S SUIT

When your opponent leads a suit that was bid by his partner, his lead does not necessarily indicate how many cards he holds.

WHEN YOUR OPPONENT LEADS A SUIT NOT BID BY HIS PARTNER

Against a Notrump Contract

When the lead is an honor card, it is probably an attacking lead from a long, strong suit.

Occasionally it may be from a 3-card suit headed by 2 or 3 honors in sequence.

When the lead is a card lower than an honor, it is most often the fourth best card from a long suit.

Sometimes, however, it is the top of a worthless 3-card suit.

The Nine is almost always top of nothing; the Eight most often is; the Seven frequently is.

Against a Trump Contract

When the lead is an honor card, it is probably an attacking lead from a 4-card or longer suit.

Occasionally it is a protecting lead from a 3-card suit headed by 2 honors in sequence.

When the lead is a card lower than an honor, it is most often the top of a worthless doubleton. Frequently, however, it is the top of a worthless 3-card suit. Occasionally it is a fourth best lead.

WHEN NO CLUES TO DISTRIBUTION ARE AVAILABLE

When neither the bidding nor the opening lead has given you any clues to the distribution of the cards your opponents hold in a suit, consider the probabilities.

If your opponents together hold an uneven number of cards in a suit, their cards are probably divided between them as evenly as possible.

If together they hold an even number, one opponent usually holds 2 more cards than the other.

CLUES TO LOCATION OF HONORS AVAILABLE FROM THE BIDDING

There are 2 kinds of points in a bridge hand—points counted for honors (A-4, K-3, Q-2, J-1) and points counted for short suits (doubletons, singletons, and voids).

In the discussion below when the words "high card points" are used, they mean points counted for honors only. They do not mean the total of points counted for both honors and short suits.

OPENING BIDS

When your opponent has made an opening bid of 1 in a suit, he usually holds at least 1 honor in that suit, probably more than 1.

He usually holds a total of at least 10 high card points in his hand, probably more than 10.

OVERCALLS

When he has made an overcall in a suit, he usually holds at least 2 honors in the suit.

He usually holds a total of at least 8 high card points in his hand, probably more than 8.

When he has made a takeout double, he usually holds at least 13 high card points. He may hold a little less if he holds a doubleton, singleton, or void in the suit he has doubled. He usually holds at least 1 honor in each of the 3 unbid suits.

RESPONSES TO OPENING BID OF 1 IN A SUIT

When he has responded 1 Notrump, or when he has raised his partner's suit, he usually holds 6 to 9 high card points.

When he has bid 1 in a higher ranking suit (1 over 1), he usually holds at least 6 high card points, probably more than 6.

When he has bid 2 in a lower ranking suit (2 over 1), he usually holds at least 8 high card points, probably more than 8.

CLUES TO LOCATION OF HONORS AVAILABLE FROM THE OPENING LEAD

LEAD OF AN HONOR

When your opponent leads an honor, it is usually the highest of 2 cards in sequence; that is, the highest of 2 equal or touching cards he holds.

If the honor is lower than the King, your opponent holds the next lower card also, but he does not hold the next higher card.

If he leads the King, he also holds either the Ace or Queen, or perhaps both.

If he leads the Ace, usually he does not hold the King.

When the contract is at Notrump, if your opponent leads an honor from a suit that was not bid by his partner, he usually holds 3 honors in the suit.

LEAD OF A CARD LOWER THAN AN HONOR

Against a Notrump Contract

When a card lower than an honor is led against a Notrump contract, it is most often a fourth best lead from a suit in which your opponent holds 2 or more honors.

The Nine, however, is never fourth best; the Eight very seldom is. Usually the Eight or Nine is the top of 3 worthless cards.

Frequently even lower cards may be the top of nothing.

Against a Trump Contract

When a card lower than an honor is led against a trump contract, it is most often the top of a doubleton, or perhaps the top of 3 worthless cards.

Occasionally it may be a singleton, or a low card from a suit headed by 1 honor, or by 2 honors not in sequence.

WHEN NO CLUES TO LOCATION OF HONORS ARE AVAILABLE

When neither the bidding nor the opening lead has given you any clues to the location of your opponents' honors, consider the probabilities.

When your opponents hold 2 honors in a suit:

50% of the time they are divided between your opponents.

25% of the time both are held by the opponent on your left.

25% of the time both are held by the opponent on your right.

PLANNING HOW TO PLAY A NOTRUMP CONTRACT

After you have reviewed the bidding and analyzed the opening lead, but before you play from the dummy to the first trick, take time to plan how you will play the hand.

Begin by counting the sure tricks you can see in your hand and in the dummy. If you do not have enough to make your contract, you must find a way to develop the additional winners you need.

Frequently you can win an additional trick by a successful finesse or double finesse, or by establishing as a winner a low card in a long suit.

Sometimes there are 2 or more ways by which you might develop a winner, and you must choose between them.

ESTABLISHING A LOW CARD WINNER

Usually in order to make a Notrump contract, you must set up and cash 1 or more low card tricks before your opponents can establish their own long suit and cash its low cards for the setting tricks.

First—You must, of course, be able to take the lead away from your opponents before it is too late.

Second—You must be able to establish your own long suit without giving up the lead too often.

Therefore, in addition to the stopper you use to take the lead away from your opponents, you must hold 1 additional stopper in their suit for each time you must lose the lead before you have made your contract.

Third—Besides the stoppers you hold in your opponents' long suit you must hold a stopper in any other suit in which you are vulnerable to attack by the defenders.

CHOOSING THE SUIT TO ESTABLISH

When you hold more than 1 long suit, plan to establish the suit that will give you, with the greatest safety, the winners you need.

WITH 2 SUITS OF EQUAL LENGTH

When you hold 2 good suits of equal length, sometimes you have enough stoppers to establish one of the suits but not enough to establish the other, as in Example 1. In that case, obviously, choose the one you can establish before it is too late.

CONTRACT
3 Notrump
OPENING LEAD
Q of Hearts

You take the first trick with your Ace of Hearts. Now you have only 1 Heart stopper left. You cannot establish your Diamond suit without giving up the lead twice. This you cannot afford to do. So establish your Club suit. In so doing you will lose the lead only once. Then the rest of your Clubs will be winners.

Sometimes you hold 2 good suits equal in length, each of which you can establish. But the number of stoppers you hold will permit you to establish with safety either of the two but not both.

Establish the one that will enable you to cash the most winners after the suit has been set up and you have regained the lead.

In Example 2 establish your Spades, not your Diamonds.

CONTRACT
3 Notrump
OPENING LEAD
Q of Hearts

In both your long suits, Spades and Diamonds, you have 8 cards in your hand and the dummy combined. The Spade suit, after it has been established, will produce 4 winners; the Diamond suit will produce only 3. The Spade suit is the one to choose.

WITH 2 SUITS UNEQUAL IN LENGTH

When you and the dummy together hold 9 cards in a suit, you can force out all the cards your opponents hold in that suit 40% of the time if you lead the suit twice, and 90% of the time if you lead it 3 times.

When you hold 8 cards you can never force them out in 2 rounds, but you can 68% of the time in 3 rounds.

When you hold 7 cards, you can never clear the suit in 2 rounds, and only 36% of the time in 3 rounds.

Consequently, the suit in which you and the dummy together hold the greatest number of cards is usually the one that offers the better chance to develop the low card winners you need. Example 3 illustrates this fact.

CONTRACT
   3 Notrump
OPENING LEAD
   Q of Spades

You cannot possibly establish even 1 low Heart winner, because 1 of your opponents is sure to hold at least 4 Hearts.

There is a 40% chance that you can force out all your opponents' Clubs in 2 rounds and establish 3 low card winners in that suit. There is a 90% chance that you can force them out in 3 rounds and establish 2 winners.

As a general rule, try to establish the low card winner(s) you need in the longest suit in your hand and the dummy combined. That is, try the suit in which you and the dummy together hold the greatest number of cards.

EXCEPTIONS TO THE GENERAL RULE

This general rule should not always be followed. You should try to establish your low card winner in a shorter suit in the combined hands in situations such as those given on the next 3 pages.

1. **When you can establish more low card winners in a suit that is shorter in the combined hands than you can in your longest suit.**

   Sometimes, in the suit in which you and the dummy together hold the most cards, these cards are evenly divided between your own hand and the dummy, such as the 8 Diamonds in Example 4. At the same time there is a suit that has fewer cards in the combined hands in which the cards are unevenly divided, such as the 7 Clubs. When this is the case, you may be able to develop more low card winners in the shorter suit because you can lead it more times.

CONTRACT
3 Notrump
OPENING LEAD
Q of Spades

There is a 68% chance that your opponents' Diamonds are divided 3-2 and that you can establish 1 low card Diamond trick by leading the suit 4 times. But you need 2 low card tricks to make your contract.

If your opponents' Clubs are divided 3-3 (and there is a 38% chance that they are) you can force out all your opponents' Clubs in 3 rounds. Then, because you can lead the suit 5 times, you can cash 2 low Clubs and make your contract.

2. **When you do not have enough stoppers to establish your longest suit.**

   When you do not have enough stoppers to establish your longest suit, try to establish a shorter suit if it offers you any chance to make your contract. See Example 5.

CONTRACT
3 Notrump
OPENING LEAD
4 of Spades

In Example 5, after you get the lead with your King of Spades, do not try to establish your long Club suit. If you do, you are sure to lose the lead, and your opponents will run their Spades and set the contract. Try to establish your Diamonds. If East holds the King, you will make your contract.

3. When you must keep the lead away from a dangerous opponent.

A dangerous opponent is one who can set the contract if he gets the lead. Sometimes in order to set up your longest suit, you must take a finesse that might give the lead to an opponent who holds an established suit, as in Example 6, or to an opponent who can make a lead that might set the contract, as in Example 7. In either case, try to establish a shorter suit if it has any chance of producing the low card winners you need.

CONTRACT
3 Notrump
OPENING LEAD
K of Spades

Stop the Spades with your Ace on the third round. If you try to establish your Clubs, your contract will be set if West holds the King of Clubs. Establish your Diamonds. If West holds the King of Diamonds, you will make 4 Notrump. If East holds the King, you will still make 3 Notrump.

CONTRACT
3 Notrump
OPENING LEAD
9 of Spades

If East gets in and leads a Heart, your contract will almost surely be set. Therefore, do not try to establish your Club suit.

Try to establish your Diamonds. If East holds the King, you will be sure to make your contract unless East holds 4 Diamonds, including the King.

4. **When you can take a greater number of tricks in the 2 suits combined, counting both low card tricks and honor tricks, by establishing your shorter suit instead of your longest.**

This situation is likely to occur when you do not have enough stoppers to establish both suits, and your longest suit is headed by both the Ace and King but contains no other honors, while your shorter suit lacks the Ace—as in Example 8.

If you establish your longest suit, you will be unable to take a single trick in your shorter suit. But if you establish your shorter suit, you can always cash the Ace and King of your longest suit also.

CONTRACT
    3 Notrump
OPENING LEAD
    Q of Hearts

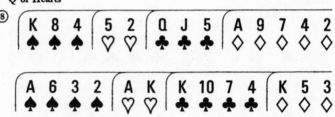

After you take the first trick, you will be able to stop your opponents' Hearts only 1 more time.

If you establish your longest suit, Diamonds, you will have to give up the lead on the third round. Your opponents will lead Hearts again to knock out your last Heart stopper; although you will regain the lead, you will win only 8 tricks (2 Hearts, 2 Spades, and 4 Diamonds). You cannot take a trick in Clubs. Your opponents' Ace will stop the first round. Then they will cash all their remaining Hearts and set the contract.

You can make your contract if you establish your Clubs instead of your Diamonds. As soon as you take the first trick, knock out your opponents' Ace of Clubs. Then, when you regain the lead with your last Heart stopper, you can take the rest of the 9 tricks you need, before you lose the lead again. You will win 2 Hearts, 2 Spades, 3 Clubs, and 2 Diamonds.

FINESSING AN HONOR
CHOOSING BETWEEN 2 FINESSES

In some deals you have 2 suits in each of which you can make a finesse that will give you another trick if the finesse succeeds. You must decide which finesse to try.

When you can make your contract by developing only 1 winner in addition to the sure tricks you hold, choose the finesse that offers the best chance of success.

When, as in Example 1, your choice lies between a simple finesse (as in the Club suit) and a double finesse (as in the Spade suit), prefer the double finesse. A simple finesse will give you the winner you need 50% of the time; a double finesse 76% of the time.

CONTRACT
3 Notrump
OPENING LEAD
9 of Diamonds

When, however, your opponents will be able to set the contract if they get the lead, as in Example 2, you cannot afford to try a double finesse. There is a 76% chance that you will lose the lead on the first round of the suit. Try to make your contract in any other way that might possibly succeed. In Example 2, take the simple finesse in Hearts instead of the double finesse in Clubs.

CONTRACT
3 Notrump
OPENING LEAD
K of Spades

If your opponents get the lead before you have taken your 9 tricks, they will cash their established Spades and set the contract.

When in order to make your contract you must develop more than 1 winner, choose the finesse which, if it succeeds, will give you all the winners you need in honor tricks and low card tricks combined. In Example 3, for instance, take a simple finesse in Diamonds instead of a double finesse in Hearts.

CONTRACT
    3 Notrump
OPENING LEAD
    Q of Clubs

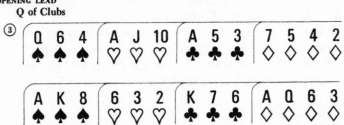

You have only 7 sure winners showing and must develop 2 more winners. There is a 76% chance that a Heart finesse will develop 1 more winner, but very little chance that it will develop 2 more. There is only a 50% chance that you can finesse your Queen of Diamonds successfully. But if the Diamond finesse does succeed, and you then lead your Ace, when your opponents' Diamonds are divided 3-2 (which they probably are) you will take a trick with 1 low Diamond as well as with your Ace and Queen.

When each of the 2 finesses available offers an equal chance of succeeding, as in Example 4, choose the one that might develop the greatest number of tricks. In Example 4, choose the Heart finesse.

CONTRACT
    1 Notrump
OPENING LEAD
    Q of Spades

You have only 5 sure tricks showing. You must develop 2 more winners. A Heart finesse or a Club finesse, either one, offers a 50% chance of succeeding. If the Heart finesse succeeds, you can develop 2 more winners. If the Club finesse succeeds, you can develop only 1 additional winner.

WHEN NOT TO FINESSE

There are times when you should avoid a finesse you would normally make, even when it is the only finesse available.

In the following situations do not finesse if there is any other line of play that offers a chance to make your contract.

1. **When you have enough sure winners to make your contract without risking a finesse.**
2. **When you can tell from the bidding or the opening lead that the finesse will probably fail.**
3. **When the finesse, if it fails, will give the lead to an opponent who is dangerous.**
4. **When, in order to take the finesse, you must use as an entry to the opposite hand a card that will be more useful to you later as an entry or stopper.**

1. **When you have enough sure winners to make your contract, as in Example 1, do not make a finesse if by so doing you might jeopardize your contract.** It is foolish to run the risk of being set for the sake of making an extra trick.

CONTRACT
  3 Notrump
OPENING LEAD
  K of Spades

You can take the 9 tricks you need to make your contract by playing out all your high cards immediately.

If you finesse the Queen of Clubs before you have taken all your 9 tricks, and East holds the King of Clubs, your opponents will get in and take enough Spade tricks to set your contract before you can take your ninth trick.

2. **When you can tell by the bidding or the opening lead that a finesse is almost sure to fail, do not risk it unless there is no other way you can hope to make your contract. In Example 2, do not finesse the Queen of Diamonds.**

CONTRACT
3 Notrump
OPENING LEAD
9 of Diamonds

②
| 6 4 3 | 5 2 | A J 10 9 6 | A Q 6 |
| ♠ ♠ ♠ | ♡ ♡ | ♣ ♣ ♣ ♣ ♣ | ◇ ◇ ◇ |

| A K 2 | A K 9 6 | Q 7 3 | 5 4 2 |
| ♠ ♠ ♠ | ♡ ♡ ♡ ♡ | ♣ ♣ ♣ | ◇ ◇ ◇ |

West's lead of the 9 of Diamonds is almost surely top of nothing, so East must hold the King. If you finesse your Queen, East will capture it and return a Diamond to knock out the Ace. Then, if he holds the King of Clubs, he will get in again and set your contract by cashing his good Diamonds.

Take the first trick with your Ace of Diamonds and you are sure to take your nine tricks even if East holds the King of Clubs.

3. **When a finesse, if it fails, will give the lead to a dangerous opponent, avoid it.**

An opponent is dangerous if he holds enough winners in an established suit to set the contract.

He is dangerous if he can lead through your Kx or Qxx in a suit in which you have no other stopper.

Try to get the winner you need in some other way.

Perhaps you can try a backward finesse in the same suit.

Perhaps there is a finesse you can try in another suit.

Perhaps you might establish a low card winner in another suit. If so, try that play even if it offers less than a 50% chance to make your contract.

4. **Do not finesse when, in order to take the finesse, you must play a card that will be more valuable to you later as an entry or as a stopper.**

a. **Do not finesse when you must use as an entry to the hand opposite your tenace position a card that you will need later as an entry in order to run a long suit.** The Ace of Hearts in Example 3 is such a card.

CONTRACT
3 Notrump
OPENING LEAD
Q of Hearts

③ | Q 6 2 | A 7 | J 10 9 5 2 | 7 5 4 |
|---|---|---|---|
| ♠ ♠ ♠ | ♡ ♡ | ♣ ♣ ♣ ♣ ♣ | ◇ ◇ ◇ |

A J 5	K 6 3 2	A Q 6	A K 3
♠ ♠ ♠	♡ ♡ ♡ ♡	♣ ♣ ♣	◇ ◇ ◇

If you play your Ace of Hearts on the first trick in order to finesse against the King of Clubs, you will have no other entry to the dummy. If your opponent holds up his King of Clubs until the third round of Clubs, you will then have no way to enter the dummy to cash your established Clubs.

You are sure to make your contract, however, if you take the first trick with your King of Hearts and then immediately lead out your Ace and Queen of Clubs. Even if the King of Clubs is not played until the third round of Clubs, you will still be able to enter the dummy with your Ace of Hearts and cash your low Clubs.

b. **Do not risk a finesse when, in order to take the finesse, you must use as an entry your only stopper in a suit that you cannot afford to leave unprotected.**

The Ace of Hearts in Example 4 is such a card.

CONTRACT
1 Notrump
OPENING LEAD
Q of Spades

④ | 6 5 4 | A 7 | J 6 5 4 | J 6 5 3 |
|---|---|---|---|
| ♠ ♠ ♠ | ♡ ♡ | ♣ ♣ ♣ ♣ | ◇ ◇ ◇ ◇ |

A K 3	6 4 3	A Q 10 7	A 4 2
♠ ♠ ♠	♡ ♡ ♡	♣ ♣ ♣ ♣	◇ ◇ ◇

Do not play your Ace of Hearts to enter the dummy in order to finesse against the King of Clubs. If you do, and your Club finesse fails, your opponents may set your contract by shifting to Hearts.

You can make your contract by immediately playing out your Ace and Queen of Clubs.

CHOOSING BETWEEN A FINESSE AND A LOW CARD WINNER

Sometimes, when you need an additional winner, there may be a possibility that you can get it either by trying a finesse or by trying to develop a low card winner in a long suit.

When the bidding or the opening lead has given you no clue as to which way offers the best chance of success, consider the odds in favor of each line of play available to you.

THE ODDS

Usually, your chances of developing a winner are as follows: Odds in favor of a finesse succeeding:

50% for a simple finesse

76% for a double finesse

Odds in favor of establishing a low card winner:

36% if you and dummy hold 7 cards in the suit

68% if you and dummy hold 8 cards in the suit

90% if you and dummy hold 9 cards in the suit

SIMPLE FINESSE VS. LOW CARD WINNER

If you hold 7 cards or more in your long suit, as in Example 1, the possibility that a simple finesse will succeed is better than the possibility that you can develop a low card winner.

CONTRACT
3 Notrump
OPENING LEAD
J of Hearts

You have 8 sure winners showing. The probabilities are that your ninth trick will come from a Spade finesse instead of a 3-3 break in Clubs. A finesse will succeed 50% of the time. When your opponents hold 6 cards in a suit, they will be divided 3-3 only 36% of the time.

If you hold 8 cards or more, as in Example 2, **try to develop a low card winner.**

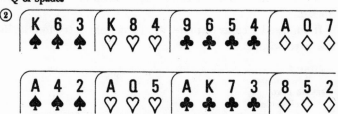

You have 8 sure winners showing. You need 1 more. There is a 68% chance that the 5 Clubs your opponents hold are divided 3-2. If they are, you can establish a low Club for your ninth trick.

There is only a 50% chance that you can finesse your Queen of Diamonds successfully against the King.

NUMBER OF STOPPERS MAY DETERMINE YOUR CHOICE

Sometimes, when you hold an 8-card or longer suit, you do not have enough stoppers in your opponents' suit to allow you to develop and cash the long suit winner you need. Before you can do so, your opponents can knock out your stoppers in their own long suit and cash their established low card winners.

In that case, of course, you must choose to finesse. Example 3 illustrates this situation.

CONTRACT
   3 Notrump
OPENING LEAD
   Q of Hearts

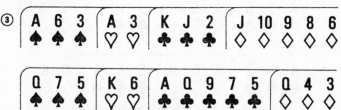

You have 8 sure winners showing, 5 Clubs, 2 Hearts, and 1 Spade. After you take the first trick, you will have only 1 Heart stopper left. You cannot establish your Diamonds without giving up the lead twice. The first time your opponents regain the lead, they will knock out your Hearts and set the contract.

Your only hope is to lead up to the Queen of Spades and finesse against the King.

DOUBLE FINESSE VS.
LOW CARD WINNER

When the choice lies between a double finesse and a long suit winner:

If you hold 8 cards or fewer, as in Example 4, try a double finesse.

If you hold 9 cards or more, as in Example 5, try to establish a low card winner.

CONTRACT
3 Notrump
OPENING LEAD
Q of Spades

④

A 5 2 ♠ ♠ ♠	A J 10 ♡ ♡ ♡	9 5 4 2 ♣ ♣ ♣ ♣	Q 6 3 ◇ ◇ ◇

K 4 3 ♠ ♠ ♠	7 6 3 ♡ ♡ ♡	A K 8 7 ♣ ♣ ♣ ♣	A K 7 ◇ ◇ ◇

You have 8 sure winners showing and must develop 1 more. There is a 68% chance that your opponents' Clubs are divided 3-2. If they are, you can establish 1 low Club trick.

There is, however, a 76% chance that you can take your ninth trick with either the Jack or Ten of Hearts if you make a double finesse. The King and Queen of Hearts will be divided between your 2 opponents 50% of the time. West will hold both the King and the Queen 24% of the time.

CONTRACT
3 Notrump
OPENING LEAD
Q of Spades

⑤

A 7 5 ♠ ♠ ♠	A 5 ♡ ♡	A J 10 ♣ ♣ ♣	8 7 5 4 2 ◇ ◇ ◇ ◇ ◇

K 6 2 ♠ ♠ ♠	K Q 8 ♡ ♡ ♡	6 4 3 ♣ ♣ ♣	A K 9 3 ◇ ◇ ◇ ◇

You have 8 sure winners showing and must develop 1 more. There is a 76% chance that you can cash either your Jack or Ten of Clubs if you make a double finesse in Clubs.

There is, however, a 90% chance that you can drive out all your opponents' Diamonds by leading the suit 3 times and establish your low Diamonds. It is not only safer to try to establish your Diamonds; it is also more profitable. The Club suit can give you only 1 more winner. The Diamond suit can give you 2.

PYRAMID YOUR ODDS

Often, after your opponents have knocked out your last stopper in their long suit, they still hold enough cards in that suit to set the contract if they can regain the lead.

Then, if you need only 1 more winner in addition to the sure tricks you have showing, you must develop that winner without surrendering the lead.

Sometimes when you are in this situation, you hold a tenace consisting of Ace-Queen or Ace-King-Jack in a short suit, which offers a 50% chance to take a trick without losing the lead. At the same time you hold a longer suit headed by Ace-King or Ace-King-Queen which offers a less than 50% chance to develop a low card winner without losing the lead.

Such a suit might be one of the following:

You and Dummy Hold	Headed by Honors	Percentage of Time Suit Will Break Favorably
7 cards	AKQ	36% of the time
8 cards	AKJ	33% of the time
9 cards	AK	40% of the time

When this is the picture, as in Examples 1 and 2, although the odds favor a finesse over a low card winner, you can increase your chances of getting the trick you need without losing the lead if you explore the possibility of a lucky break in your long suit.

If you lead out your top honors, and the suit breaks favorably, you can make your contract without risking the finesse.

If the suit does not break favorably, you can still try the finesse. The chances of the finesse succeeding will still be 50%.

CONTRACT
   3 Notrump
OPENING LEAD
   Q of Hearts

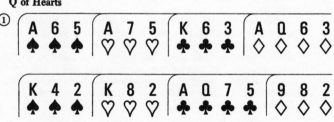

An explanation of Example 1 is given on the next page.

You have 8 sure winners showing. You need 1 additional. There is a 36% chance that your opponents' Clubs are divided 3-3 and that you can set up your 5 of Clubs as your ninth winner.

There is a 50% chance that you can finesse your Queen of Diamonds successfully.

You can pyramid your chances of making your contract by first leading out your Ace, King, and Queen of Clubs. If your opponents' Clubs are divided 3-3, your 5 of Clubs will be your ninth trick.

If your opponents' Clubs are not divided 3-3, you can still try your Diamond finesse. The chances are that it will succeed 50% of the time.

Postpone your Diamond finesse until the next to last trick. If it succeeds, you will make your contract. If it fails, you will go down 2 tricks.

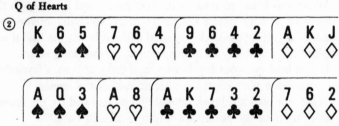

You have 8 sure winners showing. There is a 50% chance that you can finesse the Jack of Diamonds successfully for your ninth trick. But there is no way of knowing whether the finesse will succeed until you try it. If it fails, your opponents will run their established Hearts and set the contract.

There is only a 40% chance that your opponents' Clubs are divided 2-2 and that you can establish a low Club trick without losing the lead. You can find out, however, whether the Club suit will break favorably, without losing the lead, if you lead out your Ace and King of Clubs. If your opponents' 4 Clubs fall, you can then take your established Clubs and make your contract. If your opponents' Clubs do not break 2-2, you can still finesse your Jack of Diamonds. The chances will still be 50% that the finesse will succeed.

CONSERVE YOUR STOPPERS

Do not play all your stoppers in any suit until after you have established all the winners you need to make your contract. If you must risk a finesse, as in Example 1, do so while your other suits are still guarded.

CONTRACT
3 Notrump
OPENING LEAD
9 of Hearts

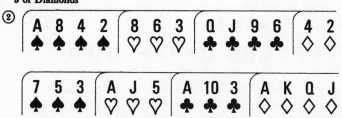

Hold up your Ace of Hearts until the third round. Then West will be out of Hearts. Take your Spade finesse before you play out your Diamonds and your Ace of Clubs. Then, if East holds the King of Spades, you will make your contract.

If you play out your Diamonds and your Ace of Clubs before you finesse, you are sure to be set. If East holds the King of Spades, you will have no way to enter the dummy to take a second Spade finesse. You will go down 1 trick.

If West holds the King of Spades, you cannot avoid going down 1 trick. But unless you still hold the Ace of Clubs to stop that suit, when West returns a Club you will be set 3 tricks.

If you must establish a long suit, drive out your opponents' stoppers in that suit before you play your high cards in other suits.

CONTRACT
3 Notrump
OPENING LEAD
9 of Diamonds

Do not use your Ace of Spades as an entry to the dummy in order to take a Club finesse. You need it to stop the Spade suit. Play out your Ace of Clubs and then your Ten to knock out your opponents' King while you still have control of all suits.

PLANNING HOW TO PLAY
A TRUMP CONTRACT

DIFFERENCE BETWEEN TRUMP AND NOTRUMP PLAY

All the methods that you use to develop winners when you are playing a Notrump contract can be used also when you are playing a trump contract.

Frequently, in either case, when you are planning how to play the hand, you must make the same decisions, such as:

Which suit to establish.

Which finesse to try.

When not to finesse.

Whether to finesse or to establish a low card winner.

There is, however, 1 important difference between trump and Notrump play.

When there are trumps, you can take tricks not only with high cards and with established low cards, but also by ruffing. Your ability to ruff makes a big difference between the way you plan to play a trump and a Notrump contract.

First, instead of counting your winners as you do at Notrump, pick out the losers in your hand.

Then plan how you can get rid of enough of them to make your contract.

> There are 4 ways you can get rid of losers:
> 1. By ruffing them with dummy's otherwise worthless trumps. See pages 30–35.
> 2. By discarding them on winning cards led from the dummy when you cannot follow suit. See page 36.
> 3. By throwing a loser on a loser. See pages 37–39.
> 4. By making an end play. See pages 40–43.

Then decide when to get rid of them. This depends upon the type of hand you hold.

HOW HANDS ARE CLASSIFIED

Type I —When you draw trumps as soon as you get the lead.

Type II —When you postpone the drawing of trumps.

Type III—When you use a combination of Types I and II.

Type IV—When you use a crossruff.

Type V —When you use a dummy reversal.

TYPE I HAND—DRAW ALL TRUMPS IMMEDIATELY

Type I is the kind of hand you hold most often when you are playing a suit contract.

As a general rule, therefore, as soon as you get the lead, draw all your opponents' trumps to prevent your high cards in other suits from being trumped. Lead trumps immediately unless you have a specific reason not to. Do this before you start to get rid of your losers.

When you hold all the top cards in the trump suit, as in Example 1, you can draw all your opponents' trumps without interruption.

CONTRACT
   4 Spades
OPENING LEAD
   K of Hearts

You have in your hand 1 losing Heart and 3 losing Diamonds. Your losing Heart will fall on the first trick. To make your contract you must get rid of 1 losing Diamond. The only way you can do this is to establish a winning Diamond in the dummy.

Be sure to draw all your opponents' trumps before you start to establish Diamonds. Otherwise one of your opponents will trump the third round.

When your opponents hold some of the high trumps, as in Example 2, they will win some tricks when trumps are led. But don't hesitate to lead trumps just on that account. Their high trumps will take tricks no matter how you play the hand.

CONTRACT
   4 Hearts
   Doubled by
   West
OPENING LEAD
   2 of Clubs

(*Explanation of Example 2 is given on the next page.*)

CONTRACT
4 Hearts
Doubled by
West
OPENING LEAD
2 of Clubs

②

| J 10 6 5 | 3 2 | 8 5 4 | A K 6 5 |
| ♡ ♡ ♡ ♡ | ♠ ♠ | ◇ ◇ ◇ | ♣ ♣ ♣ ♣ |

| Q 9 7 2 | A Q | K Q J 10 | J 8 3 |
| ♡ ♡ ♡ ♡ | ♠ ♠ | ◇ ◇ ◇ ◇ | ♣ ♣ ♣ |

Example 2—From the bidding you feel sure that West holds almost all the honor cards and at least 3 of the 5 trumps out against you. From the opening lead you assume that West's 2 is his fourth best Club, and that he holds the Queen, while East holds a Club doubleton.

Your greatest danger is that East will trump a third round of Clubs. That you must forestall.

Play a low Club from the dummy on the first trick. If your Jack wins, lead trumps immediately. You will lose the lead twice, but if the trumps break 3-2 (and the odds are 2 to 1 that they will) and East is out of trumps, you will make your contract. You will lose a Diamond trick to the Ace, but you will be able to discard a low Spade from the dummy on one of your high Diamonds and then trump your Queen of Spades with dummy's last Heart.

Sometimes you must resist the temptation to take a finesse in the trump suit in order to draw your opponents' trumps as quickly as possible. Don't risk a finesse when, if it should fail, your opponent will lead a card that his partner can trump, as in Example 3.

CONTRACT
4 Hearts
OPENING LEAD
J of Diamonds

③

| 8 5 4 3 | A 7 5 | A 8 6 | K 7 3 |
| ♡ ♡ ♡ ♡ | ♠ ♠ ♠ | ◇ ◇ ◇ | ♣ ♣ ♣ |

| A Q J 10 6 | K 4 3 | K 4 | A 9 2 |
| ♡ ♡ ♡ ♡ ♡ | ♠ ♠ ♠ | ◇ ◇ | ♣ ♣ ♣ |

You have 1 sure loser in Spades and 1 in Clubs. Even if West holds the King of Hearts you expect to make your contract. So you put up your Ace of Diamonds on the first trick in order to finesse against the King of Hearts immediately.

However, East unexpectedly drops the Queen of Diamonds on the first trick. It must be a singleton. Now you cannot afford to take the Heart finesse. If it should fail, West would lead a second Diamond which East would trump.

So lead a low trump from the dummy and take the trick with your Ace. Then lead another trump to force out your opponents' King. This line of play will insure your contract by preventing East from ruffing.

TYPE II HAND—POSTPONE DRAWING TRUMPS

There are a number of situations in which you should not lead trumps immediately, such as the following.

1. You hold losing cards in your hand that you must ruff with dummy's otherwise worthless trumps. If you draw trumps immediately, you will not leave in the dummy all the ruffers you need. See Example 1.

CONTRACT
   4 Hearts
OPENING LEAD
   9 of Diamonds

The best way you can get rid of your 3 losing Spades is to ruff them with dummy's 3 trumps. You must not lead trumps until you have done this.

2. When you have taken your first trick in one hand, but you want to lead from the opposite hand to take a finesse in the trump suit, you must postpone drawing trumps to enter that hand through an entry it holds in a side suit, as in Example 2.

CONTRACT
   4 Hearts
OPENING LEAD
   Q of Spades

Before drawing trumps, enter the dummy with your Ace of Diamonds, and then lead your Jack of Hearts for a direct finesse against the King.

3. **You cannot afford to lose the lead until you get rid of a loser, and you may not be able to draw trumps without interruption, because your opponents hold a high trump with which they might regain the lead.** For instance:

a. You hold a loser in an unguarded suit. You must discard this loser on a winning card in the dummy before your opponents get the lead again. See Example 3.

CONTRACT
  4 Hearts
OPENING LEAD
  K of Clubs

Do not draw trumps until you have discarded your 2 losing Clubs on dummy's King and Queen of Spades.

b. You hold a loser in a suit you can stop only once. Before you can get rid of this loser, you must establish a winner in the dummy on which you can discard it. To do this you must drive out a top card your opponents hold in dummy's suit. You will lose the lead when you do this. You can afford to lose the lead once, but not twice. So postpone leading trumps until you get rid of your loser. See Example 4.

CONTRACT
  4 Hearts
OPENING LEAD
  9 of Diamonds

Take the first trick in your own hand. Then, before you draw trumps, lead your Queen of Clubs to establish 2 Club winners in the dummy. If your opponent then leads a Spade, you can take the trick with your Ace and discard your low Spade on the third round of Clubs.

86

4. **When the only immediate entry to the dummy is one of the top trumps, sometimes you cannot afford to draw all of your opponents' trumps immediately.** For instance:

a. In order to make your contract, you must lead from the dummy to take a finesse in a side suit. If dummy's only entry is his high trump, you must take your finesse as soon as you play that card. If you continue to draw trumps, you will never be able to get back to the dummy again to take the finesse, as in Example 5.

CONTRACT
   4 Hearts
OPENING LEAD
   K of Clubs

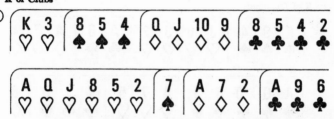

To make your contract you must finesse against the King of Diamonds. Unless you do this as soon as you play your King of Hearts, you will never be able to take the finesse.

b. You hold losers you must discard on high cards in dummy. But first you must establish those high cards as winners. If, after you have established them, you must use dummy's high trump as an entry, you cannot draw your opponents' trumps until you have discarded your losers on dummy's winners. See Example 6.

CONTRACT
   4 Hearts
OPENING LEAD
   Q of Clubs

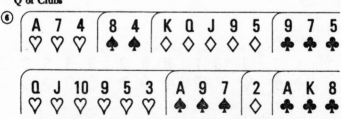

Do not draw your opponents' trumps immediately. Lead your Two of Diamonds to establish 2 Diamond winners in the dummy. Then, as soon as you recover the lead, enter the dummy with your Ace of trumps and discard losers on dummy's high Diamonds before you lead trumps.

TYPE III HAND—COMBINATION OF TYPE I AND TYPE II

When you hold a Type III hand, you start leading trumps as soon as you get in, but then stop before all your opponents' trumps are drawn, for reasons such as the following.

1. If you draw all of your opponents' trumps, you will draw all of dummy's trumps also. You cannot afford to do this because you must use 1 or more of dummy's trumps to ruff a loser you cannot get rid of in any other way, as in Example 1.

CONTRACT
4 Spades
OPENING LEAD
K of Diamonds

You cannot make your contract unless you use one of dummy's trumps to ruff your losing Club. But before you do so, draw 2 rounds of trumps to reduce the chances of an overruff.

2. If you draw all your opponents' trumps, you will have to play a high trump from dummy before all outstanding trumps are gone. The only immediate entry to dummy is his high trump.

   a. As soon as you play dummy's high trump, you must lead a side suit from the dummy to take a finesse in your own hand. If you continue to draw trumps without taking this finesse, you will never get back to the dummy to lead up to the card you want to finesse. See Example 2.

CONTRACT
4 Spades
OPENING LEAD
K of Clubs

As soon as you get in, lead your Ace of Spades. Then enter the dummy with the King of Spades and lead the Jack of Hearts for a finesse against the King of Hearts.

b. Dummy holds winners in a side suit in which you are void. As soon as you play dummy's high trump, you must lead dummy's winners and discard losers from your own hand. See Example 3.

CONTRACT
4 Spades
OPENING LEAD
K of Hearts

Take the first trick with your Ace of Hearts. Then lead your Ace of Spades and enter the dummy with your King of Spades. Lead out your 3 Club winners and discard your losing Diamond and 2 losing Hearts.

c. Before you play dummy's high trump, you must establish high card winners in the dummy on which you can discard losers from your own hand. Then as soon as you play dummy's high trump, lead dummy's winners and discard your losers. See Example 4.

CONTRACT
4 Spades
OPENING LEAD
K of Diamonds

First lead out your Ace and King of Spades. Then drive out your opponents' Ace of Clubs. When you regain the lead, use your Queen of Spades to enter the dummy so you can cash your high Clubs and discard 3 of your losing Hearts.

3. **You start leading trumps, but they do not break as favorably as you had hoped. One of your opponents holds the master trump; that is, the highest trump left. When this is the only trump outstanding against you, as a general rule stop leading trumps and switch to a side suit.** You hope that your opponent will have to ruff with the master trump and be unable to use it to draw any of the trumps left in your hand and the dummy. Example 5 illustrates this situation.

CONTRACT
    4 Spades
OPENING LEAD
    K of Diamonds

⑤

| 8 7 3 ♠ | K 6 5 ♡ | A K 5 ♣ | 8 7 5 4 ◊ |

| A K 10 9 4 2 ♠ | A 8 ♡ | 10 9 8 7 ♣ | 6 ◊ |

Lead out your Ace and King of Spades. If your opponents' trumps are divided 3-1 and either the Queen or the Jack does not fall, switch to Clubs. You hope to trump one of your losing Clubs before your opponent who holds the high trump can get the lead and draw dummy's last trump.

Occasionally, when the trumps do not break as favorably as you had hoped, and an opponent holds the master trump, it is necessary to continue to lead trumps to drive out your opponent's high trump.

This is the case when the dummy has a solid suit that he can run without losing a trick, but you can enter the dummy only once, as in Example 6.

CONTRACT
    4 Spades
OPENING LEAD
    K of Hearts

⑥

| 10 4 ♠ | 8 5 4 2 ♡ | A K Q J ♣ | 7 5 2 ◊ |

| A K 9 7 5 2 ♠ | A 7 6 ♡ | 4 ♣ | A 9 6 ◊ |

Take the first trick with your Ace. Then lead trumps. Unless both the Queen and the Jack fall, continue leading trumps. You can get to the dummy only once. So you must drive out the master trump in order to run your Clubs without interruption and discard your 3 losing Diamonds.

Sometimes there are 2 trumps still outstanding against you, both of which are higher than the best trump you have left. In that case it is often best to lead 1 of your remaining trumps, hoping that the 2 outstanding trumps will fall on the same trick. Even if one opponent holds both of the high trumps, this play does not often cost you a trick. Those 2 trumps will take 2 tricks no matter when they are played. See Example 7.

CONTRACT
    4 Spades
OPENING LEAD
    Q of Hearts

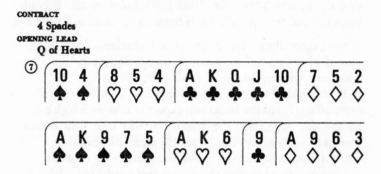

Take the first trick with your Ace of Hearts. Then lead out your Ace and King of Spades. If neither the Queen nor the Jack falls, continue with a low Spade. If the Queen and Jack both fall on this trick, you will not make your contract.

TYPE IV HAND— THE CROSSRUFF

You crossruff when, instead of drawing trumps, you use the trumps in both hands separately to ruff back and forth, one suit in the dummy and another in your own hand.

The opportunity to crossruff successfully does not occur often. It requires a freak deal—ideally, one in which each hand holds a void in a suit in which the other hand holds losers, or else it holds a singleton and the opposite hand holds the Ace, as in Example 1.

You cannot always tell at first glance whether a hand should be played as a crossruff or whether trumps should be drawn and additional winners set up in a side suit.

To determine whether a hand can be played successfully by crossruffing, count the tricks you expect to take with high cards in all the side suits, plus the tricks you will take with dummy's trumps by ruffing, plus those you will take with your own trumps. The total must be enough to let you make your contract.

Then make sure that you have sufficient entries in both hands to get back and forth as often as necessary. The entries may be either the trumps themselves or top cards in other suits. See Example 1.

CONTRACT
   5 Diamonds
OPENING LEAD
   Q of Hearts

You expect to take 3 tricks with your high cards in side suits (the Ace of Clubs and the Ace and King of Hearts); 3 tricks by ruffing Clubs with dummy's trumps; and 5 tricks with your own 5 trumps. In this way you will take 11 tricks, enough to make your contract.

You can get back and forth between the 2 hands without any difficulty by using your high Hearts and Club for entries and by crossruffing Clubs and Spades.

Sometimes, before you can start crossruffing, you must eliminate from your hand or from the dummy the last card it holds in the suit you must ruff, as in Example 2; or you must establish in a side suit a high card winner you will need to fulfill your contract, as in Example 3. When you prepare for a crossruff in this way, you usually lose the lead.

A crossruff is seldom successful if you have to give up the lead more than once before you can crossruff without interruption. Each time your opponents get in, they will lead a trump and cut down by 1 the number of tricks you can ruff in each hand.

CONTRACT
4 Spades
OPENING LEAD
Q of Hearts

Before you can start to crossruff, you must give up a Diamond trick. When your opponent takes the lead, he will lead a trump. This will reduce the number of ruffers you hold in each hand to 3 instead of 4. But you can still make your contract by cashing your Ace of Clubs and your Ace and King of Hearts and by crossruffing 3 Clubs and 3 Diamonds.

CONTRACT
5 Diamonds
OPENING LEAD
Q of Hearts

Before you can start your crossruff, you must lead a Club to establish your Queen of Clubs as a winner. Your opponent takes the first Club trick and leads a trump. You win that trick and then take 2 more high card tricks with your King of Hearts and your Queen of Clubs. You discard dummy's last Heart on your Queen of Clubs. Then dummy trumps 1 Club and 2 Hearts. You trump 4 Spades. You take 11 tricks and make your contract.

When you plan to crossruff 2 suits and you hold top cards in the third side suit, as in Example 4, cash these high cards before you start crossruffing, unless you need them to help you get back and forth between the 2 hands. If you must use them for entries, play them before you use a trump entry in the same hand. Be sure to play them before an opponent starts to discard from that suit.

If you save the top cards you hold in the third suit (the suit you do not plan to trump) until the end of the hand, you will almost never be able to cash them.

By the time you have finished crossruffing, your trumps and dummy's trumps are usually gone. Your opponents, however, still hold all the trumps they were dealt.

Meanwhile, one of your opponents has not been able to follow suit on the last 1 or 2 rounds of a suit you have been ruffing, and yet he has not been able to overtrump you. So he has been discarding from the suit in which you hold the top cards. Consequently he is able to trump these high cards if you wait until the end of the hand to lead them.

Even when you cash your high cards before you start your crossruff, don't try to take more than 2 such tricks in a suit. If you do, you may expect the third to be ruffed.

Likewise, and for the same reason, **when you hold the top card in one of the suits you plan to ruff, play it before you start trumping your low cards in that suit.**

CONTRACT
  6 Spades
OPENING LEAD
  10 of Clubs

This is an ideal hand for a crossruff. You can trump dummy's 4 losing Clubs, and dummy can trump your 3 losing Hearts. But if you do your crossruffing before you play your Ace and King of Diamonds, your Ace and King will be trumped when you lead them at the end of the hand. Your opponents will still hold trumps, and one of them will have discarded all his Diamonds.

When you crossruff, you will very seldom be overruffed if you trump low on the first or second round of a suit. But you are very likely to be overruffed if you trump with a low card on the third round. The risk of being overtrumped increases with each succeeding round.

Therefore, **start trumping with your lowest card in each hand.**

In Example 5 you will have to use all 4 of dummy's trumps to ruff your 4 losing Spades. So the first time dummy ruffs a Spade, use the Two of Hearts. If you ruff with it later, East will overtrump it. Likewise, the first time you ruff one of dummy's Clubs, use your lowest Heart.

CONTRACT
6 Hearts
OPENING LEAD
K of Spades

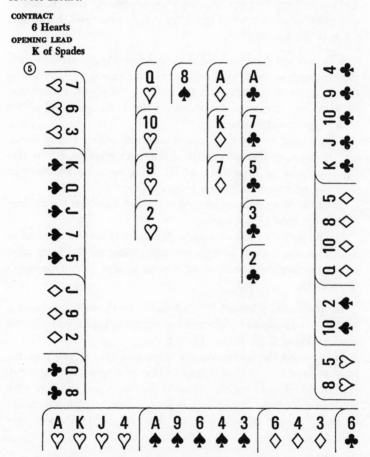

Example 5 also illustrates the importance of cashing your Ace and King of Diamonds before you start crossruffing. If you don't, by the time you have finished crossruffing, West will have discarded his 3 Diamonds but will have 3 trumps left. Your Ace and King of Diamonds will never take a trick.

TYPE V HAND—THE DUMMY REVERSAL

When you hold a Type I, II, or III hand, as you usually do, you look for an opportunity to use dummy's trumps to ruff losers you hold in your own hand. However, you avoid ruffing dummy's losers with your own trumps except when you must do so to stop the suit, or to enter your own hand, or to help establish low card winners in dummy's long suit, on which you can discard your own losers.

When you hold a Type V hand, however, you reverse the normal procedure. You ruff dummy's losers with your own trumps and use dummy's trumps to draw your opponents' trumps. You do this even when there are more trumps in your own hand than there are in the dummy.

A Type V hand occurs so seldom that the average player hardly ever recognizes the opportunity to use the dummy reversal. The expert, however, realizes that the best way to play the hand may be to reverse the dummy, whenever the hand meets all of the following requirements:

1. You hold a loser that you cannot ruff with a trump in the dummy, or discard on one of dummy's winners, if you play the hand as Type I, II, or III. Also, your hand cannot be played successfully as a crossruff (Type IV).
2. You hold a singleton or void in the suit in which the dummy holds most of his losers.
3. The dummy holds enough high trumps to let you draw all of your opponents' trumps without giving up the lead, after you have used most of your own trumps to ruff dummy's losers.

To determine whether it is advisable to reverse the dummy, begin by counting the tricks you can expect to take if you play the hand as Types I, II, III, or IV.

Then count the tricks you can expect to take if you play the hand as Type V. Count the tricks you can win with high cards you hold in side suits in both hands. Add the tricks you can take with your own trumps by ruffing dummy's losers, plus the tricks dummy's trumps will take when they are used to draw your opponent's trumps.

96

You may find that a dummy reversal will give you the most tricks in one of the following ways.

1. If by ruffing enough of dummy's losers, you reduce the number of trumps you still hold to fewer than those in the dummy, you will add an extra trick to those your combined trump suit would otherwise produce.

Then when you lead dummy's trumps to draw your opponents' trumps, and you can no longer follow suit, you can discard the loser you could not otherwise get rid of. See Example 1.

CONTRACT
4 Hearts
OPENING LEAD
9 of Spades

①

A 10 9 ♡ ♡ ♡	A K 2 ♣ ♣ ♣	A 7 6 ◇ ◇ ◇	8 7 4 2 ♠ ♠ ♠ ♠

K Q J 7 3 ♡ ♡ ♡ ♡ ♡	9 8 7 ♣ ♣ ♣	J 8 5 4 2 ◇ ◇ ◇ ◇ ◇

This hand has all the characteristics of a Type V hand.

a. You cannot get rid of your losing Diamonds by ruffing with dummy's trumps. If you try to set up a ruffing situation in the dummy, your opponents will lead trumps each time they get the lead.

b. You are void in Spades, the suit in which the dummy holds most of his losers.

c. The dummy holds enough high trumps to draw all your opponents' trumps, provided they break 3-2. The odds are 2 to 1 that they will be so divided.

You can make your contract if you reverse the dummy. You can take 3 tricks with your top cards in Clubs and Diamonds; 4 tricks by ruffing dummy's Spades; and 3 tricks when you use dummy's trumps to draw your opponents' trumps. These 10 tricks will give you your game.

To avoid an overruff and to avoid blocking your trump suit, ruff the first round of Spades with a low trump. Then ruff the next 3 rounds with your King, Queen, and Jack.

2. **If you can ruff enough losers in dummy's long suit without being overruffed, and then use dummy's trumps to draw your opponents' trumps without being interrupted, you may be able to establish and cash all the winners you need in dummy's long suit. See Example 2.**

CONTRACT
4 Spades
OPENING LEAD
K of Hearts

When the dummy goes down, at first glance this hand looks hopeless. Then you notice that it has the characteristics of a dummy reversal. You hold a singleton Club, the suit in which dummy holds most of his losers. Dummy's trumps are long enough and strong enough to draw all your opponents' trumps if they break 3-2. The odds are 2 to 1 that they will.

If you reverse the dummy by trumping 2 rounds of dummy's Clubs, you can establish 2 low card Club winners.

In your own hand you will take 1 trick with your Ace of Hearts, and 2 Spade tricks when you trump 2 rounds of Clubs. In the dummy you will take 3 Spade tricks when you draw your opponents' trumps, and 4 Club tricks. These 10 tricks will make your contract.

You must, however, be careful to use high trumps when you ruff Clubs. Also, you must lead a high trump from your own hand and overtake it to reenter the dummy. In this way you will be sure to cash your 2 established low Club winners.

Before you decide to reverse the dummy, make sure that you can get back and forth between your own hand and the dummy as often as necessary.

You may have to trump with one of your own top trumps, not only to avoid being overruffed, but also to keep from blocking the trump suit after you no longer hold as many trumps as the dummy. This is the case in Examples 1 and 2.

Unless the dummy has plenty of entries in the side suits, before you finish ruffing dummy's losers, you may have to play a round (or two) of trumps and take the trick with one of dummy's high trumps, in order to lead another of dummy's losers for you to trump. This is the case in Examples 1 and 2.

THE CARD TO PLAY
FROM DUMMY ON
THE FIRST TRICK
AGAINST A NOTRUMP CONTRACT

After the opening lead has been made and the dummy exposed, you analyze the bidding and the opening lead, plan how to develop the winners you need, and decide whether you must hold up on the first trick. Then, and not until then, you consider which card to play from the dummy on the first trick.

A declarer will make a mistake in the play of the hand more often on Trick One than at any other time.

THE NOW-OR-NEVER PLAY

Sometimes an honor in the dummy is so poorly guarded that either it will be captured or it will fall under your own higher honor unless you play it on the first trick. But it may have a chance to win a trick if you play it immediately. Such an honor should usually be played on the first trick.

This is the case in Examples 1, 2, 3, 4, and 5. In each of these examples your opponents' opening lead is the Four.

Unless you play dummy's honor at once, it can never take a trick.

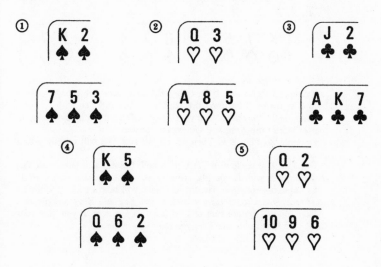

HOLD UP DUMMY'S HONOR TO
ESTABLISH ADDITIONAL WINNER

Sometimes dummy holds an inadequately guarded honor that does not call for a now-or-never play, although at first glance you are likely to think it does.

This is the case when, by holding up dummy's honor on the first trick, you may establish it as a second round winner, or you may establish an honor in your own hand that would not otherwise take a trick.

This situation is illustrated in Examples 1, 2, 3, 4, 5, and 6. In each of these examples your opponents' opening lead is the Four.

Play low from the dummy on the first trick.

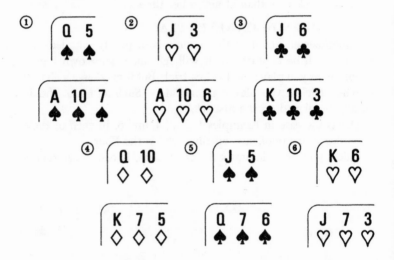

Example 1—Play low. If East plays the King, your Ace and Queen will both take tricks. If he plays the Jack, your Ace and Ten will.

Example 2—Play low. Then your Ace and Ten will both take tricks, no matter where the King and Queen are located.

Example 3—Play low. Then your King and Ten will usually win 2 tricks.

Example 4—Play low. If West holds both the Ace and Jack, your Ten and King will win. If you play your Queen, you can take only 1 trick.

Example 5—Play low. Then your Queen will take a trick. If you play your Jack, you cannot take a trick if the Ace and King are divided.

Example 6—You are sure of 1 trick if you play low. If you play your King, and East holds the Ace, you may take none.

FINESSE WITHOUT RISK
OF LOSING AN HONOR

Sometimes by playing low from the dummy you can finesse a card you hold in your own hand without the risk of losing it. Your own card will force your right-hand opponent to play a higher honor, or your card will take the trick.

This is the situation in the following examples. The opening lead in each is the Five.

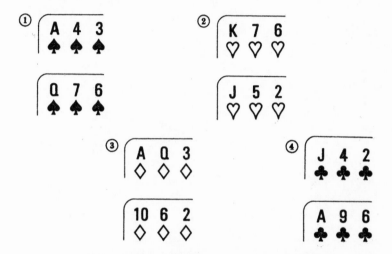

Example 1—Play low from the dummy and both your Ace and Queen will take tricks, no matter which opponent holds the King. If you play your Ace on the first trick, your Queen will not take a trick if West holds the King.

Example 2—Play low from the dummy, and you are sure to take 1 trick, no matter where the Ace and Queen are located. If you play your King on the first trick, you will not take a single trick when East holds the Ace and West holds the Queen.

Example 3—Play low from the dummy for a double finesse. You will make at least 2 tricks unless East holds both the King and the Jack.

Example 4—Play low for a triple finesse, and pray that West holds the Ten. When he does, unless East holds both the King and Queen, you will take a trick with either your Nine or your Jack besides the one you take with your Ace. When East holds the Ten, you do not gain a trick by this deep finesse.

AGAINST A TRUMP CONTRACT

When a trump has been led, play from the dummy as you would against Notrump.

When a side suit has been led in which you or the dummy holds a doubleton and can trump the third round, there is usually no reason to hold up dummy's honor. A now-or-never play is almost always best.

Part II
Summary

PERCENTAGES

WHEN YOUR OPPONENTS HOLD ONLY 1 HONOR IN A SUIT

50% of the time it is held by the opponent on your left.

50% of the time it is held by the one on your right.

It is probably held by the one who holds the greater number of cards in the suit.

WHEN YOUR OPPONENTS HOLD 2 HONORS IN A SUIT

50% of the time they are divided between your 2 opponents.

25% of the time both are held by the one on your left.

25% of the time both are held by the one on your right.

WHEN YOUR OPPONENTS HOLD AN EVEN NUMBER OF CARDS IN A SUIT

The odds are about 2 to 1 that these cards are not divided evenly between your 2 opponents.

Exception: When only 2 cards are out against you, 52% of the time they are divided 1-1.

WHEN YOUR OPPONENTS HOLD AN UNEVEN NUMBER OF CARDS IN A SUIT

The odds are about 2 to 1 that they are divided as evenly as possible.

HOW TO TAKE TRICKS WITH LOW CARDS

To develop a low card winner, lead the suit until your opponents have played all their cards that are higher than your own low card(s).

When you and the dummy hold only 6 cards in a suit, you can almost never develop a low card winner.

When you and the dummy hold 7 cards, you usually cannot develop a winner.

When you and the dummy hold 8 cards, you usually can develop a winner.

HOW TO TAKE TRICKS WITH HONORS OF EQUAL VALUE

When you and the dummy together hold a solid sequence of honors, and 1 hand contains more cards in the suit than the other, play all the honors in the shorter hand before you play the last low card in that hand.

THE FINESSE

INDIRECT FINESSE

When you try to take a trick with an honor, lead up to it if there is a higher honor outstanding.

DIRECT FINESSE AGAINST A KING

As a general rule, try a direct finesse only when you and the dummy hold all the honors except the King.

Exceptions: When your opponents hold both the King and the Ten, try a direct finesse under the following conditions:

1. Two tricks in the suit are all you need to make your contract.
2. You can trump the third round of the suit.
3. In place of the Ten you hold the Nine; and if the honor you lead is covered by the King (which in turn is captured by your Ace), you will still hold a Jack-Nine, or a Queen-Nine tenace, through which you can finesse against the Ten.

DIRECT FINESSE AGAINST A QUEEN

Try a direct finesse only when you and the dummy hold all the honors except the Queen.

HOW TO LEAD TO A DIRECT FINESSE

When you have more than 1 card that you can lead for a direct finesse, play the lowest of such cards first.

FINESSE VS. PLAY FOR A DROP

TO CAPTURE THE KING

When you and the dummy together hold 11 cards in a suit, the King will fall 52% of the time if you play your Ace on the first round.

Nevertheless, finesse against the King under the following conditions:

1. You suspect that the King is held under the Ace.
2. You must keep the lead away from the opponent who plays second hand.

When you hold less than 11 cards in a suit, a finesse is almost always the best play.

TO CAPTURE THE QUEEN

When you hold 8 cards in a suit, the Queen will fall only 34% of the time if you play your Ace and King on the first 2 rounds.

Nevertheless, play your Ace and King when you hold both the Ace and King in one hand and the Jack in the other while your opponents hold the Queen and Ten.

When you hold 9 cards, the Queen will fall 52% of the time. Nevertheless, finesse against the Queen under the following conditions:

1. Because of the bidding you suspect that the Queen is held by the opponent who will play second hand.
2. You cannot afford to let the opponent who plays second hand get the lead.

TO CAPTURE THE JACK

When you hold the Ace, King, and Queen, divided between your hand and the dummy, as a general rule, on the first round play an honor from the hand that contains 2 of the 3 top honors.

THE POSTPONED FINESSE

AGAINST A KING

When your Ace and Queen are in the same hand, as a general rule, finesse the Queen on the first round.

When your Ace and Queen are divided between your hand and the dummy, as a general rule, postpone your finesse and play the Ace on the first round.

Nevertheless, under the following conditions, finesse the Queen on the first round:

1. You cannot afford to lose control of the suit.
2. You will need the Ace later for an entry.

AGAINST A QUEEN

When you hold the Ace, King, and Jack, as a general rule, play your Ace on the first round and postpone your finesse until the second round.

Do not postpone your finesse, however, if you have no way to reenter the hand from which you must lead to finesse against the Queen.

When you hold the Ace and King in 1 hand and the Ten-Nine-Eight in the other, and you must make a direct finesse against both the Queen and the Jack, do not postpone your finesse.

AGAINST A JACK

When you hold the Ace, King, Queen, and Ten, postpone your finesse until it is your last chance to lead from the hand opposite your Ten.

THE DOUBLE FINESSE

IF ALL YOUR HONORS
ARE IN 1 HAND

When you hold the Ace-Jack-Ten, finesse the Ten on the first round and the Jack on the second.

When you hold the Ace-Queen-Ten, finesse the Ten on the first round and the Queen on the second.

IF YOUR HONORS ARE DIVIDED
BETWEEN 2 HANDS

Do not lead an honor for a direct finesse unless you can lead 1 of 3 equal cards.

CHOOSING BETWEEN A DOUBLE
AND A SINGLE FINESSE

When you hold 8 cards or fewer in the suit, as a general rule, choose a double finesse.

When you hold more than eight cards, usually choose a single finesse.

THE TRIPLE FINESSE

When you hold in 1 hand the Ace-Queen-Nine or the Ace-Jack-Nine, finesse the Nine on the first round and your Queen (or Jack) on the second.

THE BACKWARD FINESSE

You and the dummy hold all the honors in a suit except the Queen, with the Ace in one hand and the King in the other.

As a general rule, play your top honor in the short hand first. Then lead toward your long hand and finesse against the Queen.

In the following situations, however, finesse in the opposite direction:

1. Something in the bidding or the previous play makes you think that a finesse in the normal direction will not succeed.
2. You cannot afford to lose the lead to your opponent who sits behind your tenace in the long hand.

THE 2-WAY FINESSE

You and the dummy hold all the honors except the Queen, with the Ace in one hand and the King in the other. You have no idea where the Queen is. Lead the Jack (or its equal) from one hand to coax your second hand opponent to cover if he holds the Queen.

If, however, he plays low, go up with your top card in the opposite hand. Then lead back through your other opponent for a finesse in the opposite direction.

THE FREE FINESSE

Your opponents lead a suit in which the dummy holds an Ace-Queen tenace.

When you are void in the suit, finesse the Queen. If the finesse fails, trump the trick.

When you hold a singleton in the suit, finesse the Queen if you hold a loser in another suit, and the only way to get rid of your loser is to discard it on the dummy's Ace.

THE TRUMP FINESSE

In one hand you hold the King-Queen, or the Queen-Jack-Ten, in a side suit. In the other hand you are void in the suit.

Lead out your top honor. If it is covered, trump the trick. If it is not covered, discard a sure loser in some other suit.

THE OBLIGATORY FINESSE

You hold the King in one hand and the Queen in the other but no other honors in the suit.

Lead up to one of your honors. If it takes the trick, lead back toward the other honor, but duck and finesse a low card.

GET RID OF LOSERS

RUFF WITH DUMMY'S TRUMPS

Ruff losers you hold in your own hand with small trumps in the dummy that will fall when trumps are led.

You cannot expect to win a trick by ruffing a loser you hold in a suit in which the dummy holds more than 2 cards unless you use a high trump.

Do not, however, ruff with a high trump if you need it to draw all your opponents' trumps.

You cannot expect to draw all your opponents' trumps and still have a trump left in the dummy with which to ruff unless the dummy holds 4 trumps.

When you cannot draw all your opponents' trumps without exhausting dummy's trumps, draw all you can afford to in order to reduce the chance of a ruff or overruff.

When you do not hold enough high cards to clear your own long side suit, if possible, establish a low card winner you need by ruffing a round or two with dummy's trumps.

RUFF WITH DECLARER'S TRUMPS WITH RELUCTANCE

After you have drawn your opponents' trumps, save the trumps you have left in your own hand for entries and stoppers.

Do not use them voluntarily to ruff dummy's losers unless you do so to help establish a long suit in the dummy on which you can discard your own losers.

DISCARD LOSERS ON DUMMY'S WINNERS

When you can lead a winning card from the dummy, to which you cannot follow suit, discard a loser on the trick.

Discard your losers before you lead trumps, if you cannot draw trumps without losing the lead, under either of the following conditions.

1. You do not hold the top card in the suit from which you plan to discard.
2. Your high cards in dummy's suit must be promoted to top rank before you can discard your losers.

THROW A LOSER ON A LOSER

Let your opponents win a trick which you can trump, and discard a sure loser you hold in another suit, under the following conditions:

WHEN DECLARER CAN TRUMP

1. If you ruff, you will lose control of the trump suit.
2. If you let your opponents win the trick, the dummy will then hold the highest card left in the suit, on which you can discard another loser.

WHEN DUMMY CAN TRUMP

When the dummy can be overruffed, discard from the dummy a sure loser in another suit if thereby you can develop a ruffing position in that suit which will enable the dummy to trump a sure loser you hold.

THE END PLAY

On the third or fourth trick from the end of the hand, play a loser from both your own hand and the dummy to force a particular opponent to take the trick, when he will have to lead a card that will give you a trick you could not, or might not, otherwise take.

Make this end play when you recognize that your opponent will have to lead up to a tenace position in your hand or in the dummy; or that he will have to lead a suit that will give you a ruff and a sluff.

ENTRIES AND STOPPERS

CONSERVE YOUR ENTRIES

Whenever you will need a high card as an entry later, do not play it prematurely unless you are forced to.

Whenever you are able to take a trick in either hand, take it with your high card in the hand in which you hold plenty of entries.

CONSERVE YOUR STOPPERS

Play your stoppers only when your opponents lead the suit or when you must use your stoppers as entries.

Do not play them, if you can help it, until you have developed all the winners you need in other suits.

DUCKING

DUCK TO ESTABLISH DUMMY'S LONG SUIT

When the dummy has a long suit that you must establish, but there are no entries in the dummy outside that suit, and not enough high cards in the suit to run it without interruption, you must duck on the first round of the suit and sometimes on both the first and second rounds.

Occasionally you must duck even when the dummy holds an entry in another suit.

When you play a trump contract, usually draw trumps before you try to establish dummy's long suit.

HOLD UP WHEN PLAYING A NOTRUMP CONTRACT

When your opponents lead from a long suit that will set the contract if they can establish and run it, hold up. Do not play your stopper until one of your opponents will be unable to lead the suit again if he captures the lead.

If you are uncertain when that will be, hold up until the third round of the suit.

When your stopper consists of AJx, KQx, or KJx, play your cards in such a way that you will be sure to stop the suit on the third round.

After you have played your stopper, try to keep the lead away from the opponent who holds the remaining cards in the established suit.

HOLD UP WITH DOUBLE STOPPER

Even when you hold AKx and can stop the suit twice, hold up on the first round whenever you might have to give up the lead twice before you can develop and take the 9 tricks you need to make your contract.

DO NOT HOLD UP

Do not hold up under any of the following conditions:

1. You can take all the tricks you need immediately without giving up the lead.
2. The first trick may be your only chance to stop the suit.
3. Each of your opponents holds more cards in the suit than you hold.
4. By covering your opponent's honor on the first trick, you will promote a card in your own hand or in the dummy which will become a second winner and will stop the third round of the suit.
5. You hold the top card in all suits, but every finesse you must try, if it fails, will give the lead to your opponent who holds the established suit.
6. If you let your opponent take the first trick, he can shift to another suit in which you are more vulnerable.

HOLD UP WHEN PLAYING A SUIT CONTRACT

As a general rule, do not hold up except as follows:

1. Hold up when your opponent leads the King and your stopper is the AJx, unless he can shift to another suit against which you have no defense.
2. There is a suit (other than the one that has been led) that you can stop if one of your opponents leads it, but against which you have no defense if it is led by the other.

   Hold up if the opponent who will take the trick cannot make the lead that would set your contract; if you play your stopper, the other opponent might get in on the second round of the suit and make the killing lead.
3. Hold up when the dummy holds a doubleton in the suit and you hold the Ace and 2 or 3 small cards, 1 or 2 of which you want to trump.

111

PRELIMINARY ANALYSIS

CLUES TO DISTRIBUTION AVAILABLE FROM THE BIDDING

Any bid by an opponent indicates the number of cards he holds in the suit he has bid.

OPENING BIDS OF 1 IN A SUIT

In a major suit—at least 4 cards, probably 5.
In Diamonds—probably 4 or 5.
In Clubs—probably 3, 4, or 5.

OPENING BIDS OF 3 IN A SUIT

In a major suit—at least 6 cards.
In a minor suit—at least 6 cards, probably 7.

OVERCALLS

In a suit—at least 5 cards in the suit.
Take-out doubles—3 or 4 cards in each unbid suit.

RESPONSES TO OPENING BIDS OF 1 IN A SUIT

1 Notrump—fewer than 4 cards in any higher ranking suit or in partner's suit.
Single raise—at least 3 cards in partner's suit.
1 over 1, or 2 over 1—at least 4 cards.

REBIDS BY OPENING BIDDER

In suit he opened—at least 5 cards unless partner raised.
In a new suit—probably 4 cards.

CLUES TO DISTRIBUTION AVAILABLE FROM THE OPENING LEAD

WHEN AN OPPONENT LEADS HIS PARTNER'S SUIT

His lead does not necessarily indicate how many cards he holds.

WHEN HE LEADS A SUIT OTHER THAN HIS PARTNER'S

Against a Notrump Contract

When an honor is led, it is most often from a long strong suit. Occasionally, however, it is from a 3-card suit headed by 2 or 3 honors in sequence.

When a card lower than an honor is led, it most often is fourth best. Frequently, however, it is the top of a worthless 3-card suit.

The Nine almost always is top-of-nothing. The Eight very often is. The Seven frequently is.

Against a Suit Contract

When an honor is led, it is usually from a 4-card or longer suit. Occasionally, however, it is from a 3-card suit headed by 2 honors in sequence.

When a card lower than an honor is led, it is most often the top of a doubleton. Frequently, however, it is the top of a 3-card suit. Occasionally, it is fourth best. There is a very remote chance that it may be the lowest card from a 3-card suit headed by only 1 honor or by 2 honors not in sequence.

CLUES TO LOCATION OF HONORS AVAILABLE FROM THE BIDDING

HIGH CARD POINTS

Aces—4, Kings—3, Queens—2, Jacks—1.

OPENING BIDS

When an opponent makes an opening bid of 1 in a suit, he usually holds at least 1 honor in the suit, probably more. He usually holds at least 10 high card points, probably more.

When he makes an opening bid of 3 in a suit, he usually holds fewer than 10 high card points.

OVERCALLS

When an opponent makes an overcall, he usually holds at least 2 honors in the suit. He usually holds at least 8 high card points, probably more.

When he makes a takeout double, he usually holds at least 13 high card points. He may hold a little less if he holds a doubleton, singleton, or void in his opponents' suit. He usually holds at least 1 honor in each of the unbid suits.

RESPONSES TO OPENING
BID OF 1 IN A SUIT

When an opponent responds 1 Notrump or raises his partner's suit, he usually holds 6 to 9 high card points.

When he responds 1 in a higher ranking suit, he probably holds at least 6 high card points, probably more.

When he responds 2 in a lower ranking suit, he probably holds at least 8 high card points, probably more.

CLUES TO LOCATION OF HONORS AVAILABLE FROM THE OPENING LEAD

LEAD OF ANY HONOR

When an opponent leads the Ace, he usually does not hold the King.

When he leads the King, he usually holds either the Ace or the Queen, perhaps both.

When he leads the Queen, Jack, or Ten, he denies that he holds the next higher honor and usually guarantees that he holds the next lower card.

When he leads an honor against a Notrump contract, he usually holds 3 honors in the suit.

LEAD OF A CARD LOWER THAN AN HONOR

Against a Notrump Contract

When an opponent leads a low card, it is most often fourth best. Frequently, however, it is the top of a 3-card suit.

The Nine is never fourth best. The Eight very seldom is. The Seven occasionally is.

Against a Suit Contract

When he leads a low card, it is most often the top of a doubleton. Frequently it is the top of a 3-card suit. Occasionally it may be a singleton or a low card from a 3-card suit headed by 1 or 2 honors not in sequence.

PLANNING HOW TO PLAY A NOTRUMP CONTRACT

Begin by counting the sure winners in your hand and the dummy. If you do not have enough to make your contract, decide how to develop the additional winners you need.

DEVELOP A LOW CARD WINNER

To develop a low card winner you must be able to take the lead away from your opponents before it is too late, and you must be able to establish your low card winners without giving up the lead too often.

Besides the stoppers you hold in your opponents' long suit, you must hold stoppers in any other suits in which you are vulnerable to attack.

CHOOSING THE SUIT TO ESTABLISH

Establish the suit that will give you, with the greatest safety, the winners you need.

WITH 2 SUITS OF EQUAL LENGTH

When you hold 2 good suits of equal length, if you have enough stoppers to establish one of the suits but not enough to establish the other, choose the one you can establish before it is too late.

If the number of stoppers you have will allow you to establish either one of the two but not both, choose the one that will allow you to cash the most winners after the suit has been set up.

WITH 2 SUITS UNEQUAL IN LENGTH

When you hold 2 suits unequal in length, as a general rule, establish the longer suit in your hand and the dummy combined.

Exceptions: Establish your shorter suit in situations such as the following:

1. You can establish more winners in the shorter suit because the longer suit is evenly divided between you and the dummy, while the shorter suit is so unevenly divided that you can lead it more times.
2. You do not have enough stoppers to establish your longer suit.
3. In order to set up your longer suit you must take a finesse that might give the lead to a dangerous opponent.
4. You can take a greater number of tricks in the 2 suits combined, counting both low card tricks and honor tricks, by establishing your shorter suit.

FINESSE AN HONOR

CHOOSING BETWEEN 2 FINESSES

When you can make your contract by developing only 1 additional winner, prefer a double finesse to a simple finesse unless you cannot afford to lose the lead. A simple finesse will give you a winner 50% of the time, a double finesse 75% of the time. But there is a 75% chance that you will lose the lead on the first round of the double finesse.

When you must develop more than 1 winner, choose the finesse that, if it succeeds, will give you all the winners you need, counting honor tricks and low card tricks in both suits combined.

115

DO NOT FINESSE

Do Not Finesse in the following situations if there is any other line of play that offers a chance to make your contract.

1. You have enough sure winners to make your contract without risking a finesse.
2. You can tell by the bidding or the opening lead that a finesse will probably fail.
3. A finesse, if it fails, will give the lead to an opponent who is dangerous.
4. To take the finesse you must use as an entry to the opposite hand a card that will be more useful to you later as an entry or a stopper.

CHOOSING BETWEEN A FINESSE AND DEVELOPING A LOW CARD WINNER

WHEN THE CARDS IN THE SUIT ARE DISTRIBUTED NORMALLY

Your chances of developing an additional winner you need are usually as follows.

WHEN YOU TRY A FINESSE

50% for a simple finesse
75% for a double finesse

WHEN YOU TRY TO ESTABLISH A LOW CARD WINNER

36% if you hold 7 cards in the suit
68% if you hold 8 cards in the suit
90% if you hold 9 cards in the suit

PYRAMID YOUR ODDS

Sometimes your opponents will set the contract if they can regain the lead. You hold an AQ or AKJ tenace in a short suit, which offers a 50% chance to take a trick without losing the lead. At the same time you hold a suit headed AK or AKQ which offers less than a 50% chance to develop a low card winner without losing the lead.

You can increase your chances of getting the trick you need without losing the lead by leading out the top honors in your long suit. If the suit does not break favorably, stop and try the finesse.

PLANNING HOW TO PLAY
A TRUMP CONTRACT

First, pick out the losers in your own hand.

Second, decide how you can get rid of them.

Third, decide when to get rid of them. This decision depends on the type of hand you hold.

TYPE I HAND—DRAW ALL TRUMPS IMMEDIATELY

As soon as you get the lead, draw all opponents' trumps.

Don't risk a finesse in the trump suit when, if it should fail, your opponent will lead through a suit against which you have no defense, or one that his partner can trump.

TYPE II HAND—POSTPONE DRAWING TRUMPS

Postpone drawing trumps under the following conditions.

1. If you lead trumps immediately, you will not have left in dummy all the ruffers you need.
2. You have taken the trick in one hand, but you want to lead from the other hand for a trump finesse.
3. If you cannot draw trumps without risk of losing the lead, postpone drawing trumps under the following conditions.

   a. You have, in a suit you cannot stop, a loser which you can discard on a winning card in the dummy.

   b. You have a loser in a suit you can stop only once, but before that suit is played you must establish a high card winner in the dummy on which you can discard your loser.

TYPE III HAND—COMBINATION OF TYPE I AND TYPE II

Start leading trumps as soon as you get in, but then stop before all your opponents' trumps are drawn under the following conditions.

1. If you draw all your opponents' trumps, you will draw all dummy's trumps also; but you must use 1 or more of dummy's trumps to ruff your own losers.
2. Dummy's only immediate entry is one of the top trumps.

   a. As soon as you play dummy's high trump, you must lead

from the dummy in order to take a finesse in your own hand in a side suit; or

b. As soon as you play dummy's high trump, you must lead a winner dummy holds in a side suit in which you are void, and discard a loser from your own hand; or

c. Before you play dummy's high trump, you must lead a side suit in order to establish a winner in the dummy, on which later you will be able to discard a loser from your own hand.

3. Trumps do not break favorably and an opponent holds the master trump. As a general rule, switch to a side suit.

Continue to lead trumps, however, when dummy has a solid suit that he can run, but you can enter the dummy only once.

Usually, continue to lead trumps, also, when there are still 2 trumps outstanding, both of which are higher than your own highest trump. They may be divided and fall together.

TYPE IV HAND—
THE CROSSRUFF

To decide whether the hand should be played as a crossruff, count the tricks you expect to take with high cards in the side suits, plus the tricks you will ruff with dummy's trumps, plus those you will ruff with your own trumps.

Then make sure you have sufficient entries to get back and forth as often as necessary.

You should seldom try a crossruff if you will have to give up the lead more than once before you can crossruff without interruption.

When you hold top cards in any of the side suits, play them before you start to crossruff.

Start crossruffing with the lowest card in each hand.

TYPE V—THE
DUMMY REVERSAL

Consider using a dummy reversal if you have the following requirements:

1. You hold too many losers in your own hand to get the tricks you need if you play the hand as Type I, II, or III and your hand is not suitable for a crossruff.

2. You hold a singleton or void in the suit in which dummy holds most of his losers.

3. Dummy's trumps are long enough and strong enough to draw all your opponents' trumps.

If you find all these conditions, count the tricks you can win in each hand with high cards in side suits. Add the tricks you can take by trumping dummy's losers, plus the tricks dummy's trumps will take when you play them to draw your opponents' trumps.

If the total gives you the number you need, reverse the dummy. Ruff dummy's losers with your own trumps. Use dummy's trumps to draw all your opponents' trumps.

THE CARD TO PLAY FROM DUMMY ON THE FIRST TRICK

AGAINST A NOTRUMP CONTRACT

When an honor in the dummy is so poorly guarded that either it will be captured or it will fall under your own higher honor, as a general rule, play it on the first trick.

Exception: Play low from dummy when by holding up dummy's honor on the first trick, you will establish it as a second or third round winner, or you will establish an honor in your own hand that would not otherwise take a trick.

AGAINST A SUIT CONTRACT

When a trump has been led, play from the dummy as you would against Notrump.

When a side suit has been led, in which you or the dummy holds a doubleton and can trump the third round, there is usually no reason to hold up dummy's honor. A now-or-never play is almost always best.